TEACHING KIDS TO THINK

Raising Confident, Independent,
& Thoughtful Children in an Age
of Instant Gratification

DARLENE SWEETLAND, PhD
RON STOLBERG, PhD

sourcebooks

Published by Sourcebooks, Inc.
P.O. Box 4410, Naperville, Illinois 60567-4410
(630) 961-3900
Fax: (630) 961-2168
www.sourcebooks.com

Library of Congress Cataloging-in-Publication Data

Sweetland, Darlene.
 Teaching kids to think : raising confident, independent, and thoughtful children in an age
of instant gratification / Darlene Sweetland, Ron Stolberg.
   pages cm
 Includes bibliographical references and index.
 (trade : alk. paper) 1. Problem solving in children. 2. Frustration in children. 3. Parenting.
4. Parent and child. 5. Internet—Social aspects. I. Stolberg, Ronald A. II. Title.
 BF723.P8S94 2015
 649'.6—dc23

                                        2014035534

            Printed and bound in the United States of America.
                    VP 10 9 8 7 6 5 4 3 2 1

Contents

Introduction
The Instant Gratification Generation

As clinical psychologists, we have worked with families and educators for more than twenty years. Recently, we have found ourselves marveling at the number of children and teens who become easily frustrated when asked to solve a simple social dilemma or deal with a problem on their own. Here are only a few examples of situations we witnessed in our therapy practices the week we began writing this book:

- A seven-year-old girl became angry at her parent and screamed, "My iPad is not charged! You didn't charge my iPad!"
- A mother told her disappointed ten-year-old son, "I will call his mom and tell her that her son left you out of the handball game."
- A seventh-grade girl panicked because she forgot to study for a test, and her father said, "I will send your teacher an email and ask if you can take it a day later."
- A high school boy was unhappy about a teacher he was assigned for a history class, and his mother said, "I will call the school and see if I can get your schedule changed."

- A teenage girl grew annoyed at her mother and said, "I need the iPhone 5, not your old phone because yours is lame!"

Whether these kids were dealing with friendship confusion, an academic challenge, or a parental dispute, their responses were the same. They were upset by the situation and became increasingly angry, anxious, or even panicked when their problem wasn't solved right away. It never seemed to cross their minds to take a moment to figure out a possible solution; instead, they launched straight into meltdown mode. We observe this troubling pattern in our personal lives as well as our professional lives. In addition, parents, teachers, administrators, and coaches are all talking to us about their concerns about what they are seeing. The need for someone to solve their problem right away is rampant in many environments and talked about all the time.

More recently, this low tolerance for frustration has become a hot-button topic brought up by colleagues, friends, and family alike. It has also been highlighted in the media with articles such as "Millennials: The Me Me Me Generation" published in *Time* magazine in May 2013 and "Are We Raising a Generation of Helpless Kids?" on the Huffington Post website in February 2012.[1] The trend continues to worsen, and as child psychologists and concerned parents, we found ourselves asking the same questions over and over: What is happening with this generation of kids? Why do they expect everything to be given to them? And where did this sense of entitlement come from? We then realized that our society is enabling this low-frustration tolerance.

Every generation has faced its own challenges and has been shaped by society's expectations and pressures. The Silent Generation (born between 1925 and 1945) responded to the

Great Depression and World War II by working hard but remained quiet about protests or political opinions relative to other generations.[2] After World War II, the Baby Boomers (born between 1946 and 1964) grew up in a world of great urban development and larger families, and they believed that with hard work, the American dream would be theirs.[3] Generation X (born between 1965 and the early 1980s) experienced the introduction of the personal computer, cable television, and the Internet.[4] While identified as a highly educated group, they were more reluctant to invest as much energy as their parents in job security, retirement, and the American dream.

Now we have a generation directly impacted by the rapid development of technology. Kids born since the late 1980s and early 1990s, known as Generation Y or millennials, have known nothing other than full access to the digital world, meaning that swift communication, immediate access to information, and the ability to work from anywhere is considered normal to them.[5] Recent advancements in technology have resulted in products that are more convenient for us. Answers to questions are provided at the click of a mouse thanks to Google, directions to a new restaurant are provided via GPS, any TV show missed can be found "on demand," and people are available to solve problems instantly via cell phone. The result is that today's growing children and teens are learning to navigate the tumultuous world with the aid of all these modern conveniences—and therefore expect instant solutions to their problems.

This generation of children and adolescents has grown up with very little need to wait for anything. Not only do they expect instant solutions to their challenges, but they are also increasingly dependent on adults. Parents are doing more for their children than ever before, and technology has advanced in such a way that conveniences are no longer the exception but the rule. This generation is one of *instant gratification*.[6] Today's children expect more with less work. Supported and fueled by the rapid pace of technology, we are raising a group of kids who are being *taught not to think*. This is the first generation in history where the unique advancements and changes of our time are putting children at a disadvantage: we are failing to teach them how to solve complicated problems, cope with unexpected changes in life, and lead independent lives.

In addition, the academic expectations for our children are also higher than in any past decade. It is more difficult to get into college today than ever before, and parents begin to worry about their children's preparedness as early as preschool—will they be placed in the top reading group in kindergarten? Additionally, parents feel a lot of pressure to enroll their children in any extracurricular activity that could put them at an advantage (sports, art, languages, etc.). What if their children miss opportunities that could possibly put them ahead?

It seems like this push to excel would increase the opportunities and skills of developing children. Isn't that what it is all for? In fact, the opposite is happening. Parents are eager to provide their children with the best opportunities, but this has resulted in parents who rescue their children from making typical, developmentally expected mistakes. That means today's children aren't learning from their mistakes. For example, consider Sam. If Sam does not turn in his report on time, he will get a lower grade, but he has forgotten his report at home. Sam uses his cell phone to call his mom, and she rushes to bring the report to school. His mother thinks that if she does not bring the report, he will get a lower grade. But her panicked line of thinking continues from there. If Sam receives a low grade on his report, it will affect his semester grade, which will affect his grade point average, which will affect what college he gets into, which will affect his job choice, and so on, and so on. Parents often rationalize this behavior by saying to us, "Well, it was just that once." But is it really? Using this example, will a late paper *really* impact Sam's career as an adult? (Unlikely.) Allowing Sam to deal with the consequences of a late report on his own may prolong his struggle and frustration in the short term, but it will teach him to be independent and self-sufficient in the long run. To put it another way, consider this. Who would be a better employee, manager, or business owner—someone who makes a mistake and asks someone else to fix it, or someone who makes a mistake, takes responsibility for the mistake, and learns the skills to resolve it so it can be avoided in the future?

We wrote *Teaching Kids to Think* to help parents understand why the Instant Gratification Generation is at such a disadvantage when entering the adult world. We aim to call attention to the valuable everyday opportunities that are lost when today's youth rely too heavily on the convenience of technology or their parents to solve their problems for them—otherwise "teachable moments" that are essential to a child's social, emotional, and neurological development. We wrote this book not out of frustration toward parents but as empathetic parents ourselves who are also raising children in this generation. We, too, are learning the challenges and feel the same temptations to (unwittingly) reinforce the Instant Gratification Generation. We want to support parents in raising children who are confident, considerate, and conscientious of their community, and throughout this book, we will share ideas and techniques for preparing children of all ages with lifelong skills that will help them lead responsible and fulfilled adult lives. We will help parents identify the traps they may easily fall into as they face the unique challenges of raising children in this generation.

So what do we mean by these lost opportunities? Socially, children in this generation are missing opportunities to interface with others in a way that promotes positive interpersonal relationships. Emotionally, they are missing experiences to develop confidence in their skills and the ability to cope with unforeseen challenges. And, neurologically, they are being put at a great disadvantage in developing the ability to plan, organize, problem solve, and make decisions. In this book, we discuss how these lost opportunities relate specifically to parenting, education, and technology. In addition, we share our experiences working with families, as well as provide information gathered from in-depth interviews with administrators, teachers, coaches, and parents who have encountered the same trends. We include vignettes taken from our clinical work. The vignettes we used were chosen because the situations reflected common themes and occurred in multiple situations. We also chose them because many readers can relate to them.

In chapter 1, we begin by showing parents how to identify and overcome parent traps that are so easy to fall into in this era of ease and convenience. In chapter 2, we address the impact on children of parental intervention, which prevents children from figuring things out on their own. This is followed by chapter 3, in which we discuss the temptation parents feel to protect their children from making mistakes and how it ultimately fosters dependence in their children. Developmentally, it is very important for children to experience challenges and figure out how to overcome them. Important developmental lessons are discussed in chapter 4. Chapter 5 highlights how missed practice with making mistakes and overcoming challenges impacts a child's brain development and ability to develop planning, problem-solving, and decision-making skills. For most families, education is a primary focus, and parents feel overwhelmed with the pressure to protect their kids from missing opportunities to get ahead. In chapter 6, we address how to support and guide children without falling into the trap of rescuing them from learning how to succeed on their own. Chapters 7 and 8 provide guidelines on productive and responsible uses of technology, including the use of smartphones, video games, social media, and the Internet. The positive impact of athletics is discussed in chapter 9. Chapter 10 examines why this generation of kids is so vulnerable to substance use and what to do about it. For parents of older teens and young adults who are following the trend of the Instant Gratification Generation, chapter 11 is devoted to ways to change those patterns. Next, chapter 12 focuses on how parents often unknowingly model for their kids the need for instant gratification. We summarize in chapter 13 the lessons we hope readers have learned. Finally, throughout every chapter, we offer many tips to parents so they can positively approach these challenges and avoid falling into the parent traps.

Note: All names and identifying information used in the vignettes throughout the book have been changed to protect the identities of the people we work with.

CHAPTER 1
The Parent Traps
Do You Take the Bait?

It is open house for the third-grade class in the local ele-mentary school. Over the past two weeks, students have been working on a poster project about planets. Computer-generated graphic designs, charts, and neatly typed and formatted titles and descriptions dominate the posters on display. Only one poster board features hand-drawn pic-tures and carefully handwritten titles and descriptions. All these posters were completed to the level of a typical third-grade student. While the computer-generated figures looked neat and interesting, the handmade poster clearly took a lot of thought, effort, and planning. In addition, do you think a child is more likely to remember what a planet looks like by printing a photo from the Internet, or hand drawing it? Yet that night, the parents of that child approached the teacher, concerned that their child was not as advanced as the other students.

—Dr. Darlene and Dr. Ron

As parents, we want the best for our children. We want to provide them with guidance, support, and instruction to develop into caring and confident adults. Yet parents all across the country are also getting the message that "it is a tough world out there" and that their children need to have every advantage so they can be competitive in the college and job market. Take a moment to read that sentence again, then ask yourself whether you would answer true or false to this statement:

It is a tough world out there, and my children need to be provided with every advantage so they can be competitive in the college and job market.

That is a *parent trap*. A parent trap is a situation in which parents are drawn to solve problems for their children or rescue them in a way that ultimately stifles growth opportunities. We have seen many parent traps in our practice, where parents work harder than their children to solve the children's dilemmas or problems. Of course, you want to assist your child in any way you can. The difference is in whether you are *giving* your children advantages or *assisting* them in developing the skills that will put them at an advantage. When parents set everything up *for* their kids, they lose the chance to learn to do things on their own, which ultimately puts them at a disadvantage. On the other hand, when parents assist their children in developing skills so they can gain those advantages themselves, their children truly enter the adult world ahead of the game. With the pressures so strong in this generation, parents often fall into the trap of giving rather than assisting.

Do you fall into parent traps? Answer *true* or *false* to the following statements:

- When my children ask for something to eat, I typically stop what I am doing and get it for them.

- My child uses an electronic device to pass the time whenever she is required to wait for anything.
- If my child forgets a book for his homework, I will drive him back to school to get it.
- If all my child's friends have the latest cell phone, I will also buy one for my child.
- I have to run around getting supplies the night before a project is due, because my child waits until the last minute to work on the assignment.
- My child does fewer than two chores per day.
- My child has very little free time during the week because of all the extracurricular activities she has.
- The TV is often on in my home, because it gives my child something to do.
- I receive more than two or three texts from my child per day asking me questions, even during school hours.
- I buy something for my children when we are at the store as a reward for not putting up a fuss about going.
- If I am not at an agreed meeting place the second my child arrives there, I receive a text asking where I am.

If you answered *true* to any of these questions, you may be falling into parent traps.

It is so easy to fall into parent traps! The allure of the traps is that parents want to do the best for their kids, so it's easy to interpret a situation as "helping" the child. But the previous examples are not helping, protecting, or guiding children; they are solving problems for them.

In this chapter, you will learn how to define and identify the five most common parent traps and learn strategies on how you can avoid them in the future. The following chapters will then illustrate in more detail how these traps apply to specific events or situations in a child's life and the relationship between these traps and parenting. Included in those chapters are guidelines to help parents establish appropriate expectations for their children and teens at different developmental levels.

The five most common parent traps are as follows:

- **The Rescue Trap:** Parents rescue their children from their problems.
- **The Hurried Trap:** Parents meet their children's needs quickly, not requiring them to be patient and wait.
- **The Pressure Trap:** Parents push children forward too fast.
- **The Giving Trap:** Parents give children something without them earning it.
- **The Guilt Trap:** Parents react impulsively because they feel guilty or unsure.

The Rescue Trap

Parents hate to see their children struggle. As a result, parents often feel compelled to "save" their children from a negative experience by fixing their problems for them. The consequence of this parental behavior is children's learned expectation that things will be done for them. This denies children the opportunity to solve problems themselves.

Everyone agrees that one of the best lessons a child can learn is the ability to think and problem solve on his or her own. Childhood is full of opportunities to routinely practice these skills, but there are two areas in which parents often fall into the trap of rescuing their children from their struggles: academics and social relationships.

Academics

Academics are one area where the rescue trap can catch people. Parents get caught up in the hysteria that every grade and every assignment will impact their child's chances of getting into a choice college. This fear leads parents to attempt to rescue their children, which results in the parents avoiding very important teaching opportunities. For example, a seventh-grade history teacher recently shared with us a situation with a student who failed a test because he did not study. The teacher received a call from the mother of the student who asked what her son could do to raise his grade, to which the teacher replied, "Study." The mother then asked if there was any extra credit her child could do, to which the teacher told her that her son had not participated in any of the extra credit opportunities given throughout the quarter. She asked if her son could have the option of completing the extra credit late, and the teacher said he could not. She sounded confused and said, "Then how can he pull up the grade?" And the teacher again said, "Study for the next test." The student in question did not work hard although he was challenged by the class. This scenario involved a student who was doing minimal work and a parent who saw the letter grade as more important than the skills learned *earning* the grade. This parent had good intentions—to make something easier for her son—but missed a valuable opportunity to teach him the importance of hard work, not to mention planning, organization, and responsibility, because she was focused on the objective grade. In addition, the parent was clearly working harder than the student to resolve the student's problem.

When parents provide children with the solutions to dilemmas, they are teaching them that problems are solved by asking someone else for the solution. Instead of focusing on a quick fix to raise his grade, which wasn't deserved, this mom could have focused on his lack of effort, planning, and responsibility. He would then experience the natural consequences of getting a low grade in the class, such as loss of privileges until his grade is brought up. His parents could then discuss how to do it differently the next time.

Social Situations

Another area we see parents commonly falling into the rescue trap is when they see their children struggling with their peers. Whether their children have a peer conflict or parents feel like their children are being excluded, even the most well-intentioned parents find themselves trying to resolve their children's peer issues rather than let them work the issues out on their own or helping their children come up with a resolution. If parents are always in charge of their children's social calendars, it doesn't help them learn to develop friendships on their own. This trap applies as much to preschool play groups as it does to adolescent dating habits. Parents have ideas about what they want their children's social life to look like, but that may not be in line with their children's interests. In the short term, the child may feel included, but in the long term, the child hasn't learned the social skills needed to make and keep friends. A parent's role is to guide their children and teach them how to maintain friendships, not do it for them.

Most parents will agree that there are ups and downs when developing friendships and that children need to learn how to deal with social challenges on their own, such as how to deal with disagreements or gossip. Yet the temptation to make a situation better for their child is so strong that parents can't help themselves from intervening—for example, they start calling the parents of the other children, setting up apologies, and forcing children to be friends again. Most parents don't even realize they have fallen in the trap. This situation is quite common for parents.

Parents attempt other social rescues too. These include buying children the top brand-name clothes or electronic gadget so they will be accepted by their friends. When parents simply purchase things for their children because their child says "all the other kids" have them, parents are rescuing their children from a chance to figure out how to deal with a social dilemma—in this case, feeling left out among their peers. Instead, parents should give their children the opportunity to rescue themselves and become their own problem solvers.

Give Children the Opportunity to Rescue Themselves

In the short term, it feels great to make your child feel better. It will feel even better for both of you when you teach your child how to resolve common social issues on her own. As parents, we have had a lot of practice solving problems, and it may come easy to us. Children need opportunities for their own practice. To teach them this skill and help their self-confidence, we offer the following suggestions.

- Start by resisting the temptation to "make everything all right." Give your child the opportunity to solve the problem himself.

- With elementary school–age children, it might be helpful to talk with them about multiple possible solutions, just like a multiple-choice test. Ask which one of the solutions they would like to try, based on their age and development. Either let them try it or help them implement the solution.
- With middle school–age children, it is important to let them develop their own set of possible solutions and then ask them to share with you the strengths and weaknesses of each before they decide how to proceed. Your feedback and support is important here.
- With high school–age children, you really need to be available for emotional support, but much of the problem solving must come from the child.

The Hurried Trap

Parents want to do everything in their power for their children, and that translates into feeling pushed to meet their needs quickly. In doing so, they enable a pattern of instant gratification.

For many parents, caring for children often seems to translate into meeting their needs quickly. If their child wants something and they provide it immediately, their child is satisfied and happy. However, this pattern strengthens the expectation for instant gratification. This pattern is easy to spot in today's children and adolescents, who seem unwilling to wait for anything, ever!

"Good things come to those who wait" has been touted as an important life lesson for decades. However, what is the relevance in today's competitive world? When high academic achievement and a student's acceptance into a "competitive" college are top priorities for many parents, how does this lesson of patience relate to the ultimate goal?

Walter Mischel, a psychologist who is well known for his research on delayed gratification and children, is most noteworthy for the Stanford marshmallow experiment (reported in an article coauthored by Ebbe Ebbesen).[1] In the study, he offered children a choice of eating one marshmallow that was placed in front of them immediately or two if they were able to wait (approximately fifteen minutes). He then compared the children who were able to wait to the children who were not able to wait to eat the marshmallow, a unique measure of delayed gratification. He followed up with these children eighteen and twenty years later and found that the children who were able to delay gratification ultimately did better academically and earned higher SAT scores.[2] Similar studies found better social responsibility and higher achievement strivings.[3] Overall, research shows that students who were able to delay gratification were more likely to focus on an academic goal and work toward it. A student who is able to delay gratification is able to plan a carefully considered approach, as opposed to acting impulsively based on an initial desire. A big part of our work with children involves getting them to stop just long enough to think before they act. Clearly, teaching children self-discipline and delayed gratification is paramount in helping them achieve academic goals and develop positive interpersonal skills.

When Children Focus on Getting Their Own Needs Met First

In my practice one day, I met with a teenage girl and her mother. The girl came in very upset and said, "Dr. Darlene, my mom is so unfair! I was planning a sleepover with my friends all week where we were going to do each other's makeup, hair, and do facials, and my mom almost ruined it."

It turns out her parents didn't know about the sleepover or how much effort it would require to purchase the specific beauty supplies from several different stores. The Friday afternoon of the sleepover, the girl sent her mother a text saying she needed her mom to take her to the store to buy supplies. Mom did not see the text because she was at an appointment. Later that night, the girl yelled at her mother for ruining the sleepover, because she would not have time to get the supplies before her softball practice. The mom ended up going to several stores and canceling her afternoon plans so that she could immediately meet her daughter's needs, which were poorly planned in the first place.

—Dr. Darlene

Children and teens in the Instant Gratification Generation tend to consider themselves as individuals, as opposed to a part of a family unit. When children expect something right away, they don't consider the impact meeting that need quickly might have on others. In the previous example, the girl did not consider why her mother did not see the text or that the family may have had other plans that evening. She simply assumed her mother would do as she asked in regard to her event. The girl considered only her own schedule and needs.

Parents can inadvertently encourage this expectation when they don't make their children wait for anything. If a child is always the primary focus and his needs are constantly met first, it is fair for the child to expect that this will always be the case. Why wouldn't he? And when the time comes that the parents cannot meet his needs right away, it makes sense that the child will become angry and demand attention. He is not thinking about *why* the parent can't do something, because he is not used to considering himself within a family unit. Therefore, the time spent waiting can feel uncomfortable.

⁎Teaching children to feel comfortable with waiting (in other words, patience) is the key to teaching delayed gratification. This technique works even with young children. To help children consider others and develop patience, parents need to regularly communicate that their child will have to wait. If a five-year-old child says, "Mom, can you play with me?" Mom can say, "I can play with you in a few minutes, after I finish folding the laundry." If an eight-year-old child says, "Dad, can you make us lunch?" Dad can say, "I will be ready to make it in ten minutes." Children will learn to either wait or get what they want by themselves. Both are great options. This teaches children not only the quality of patience but also that they are part of a family or community and the needs of everyone should be considered. In addition, they may develop a level of self-sufficiency and self-confidence, by doing something constructive as they wait. This is such a simple thing to do and such a wonderful lesson to teach.

Make Them Wait

If you are engaged in something and your child makes a request, develop an automatic response to let her know what you are doing and how long she will have to wait for you to meet that request. For example, say, "I'd love to help you with that. Let me finish what I am doing and I will be with you in a few minutes."

Even if you are available to meet your child's request at the time she asks, regularly have her wait. The younger your child is, the shorter the waiting period. It is also great to share a reason with your child for why she is waiting; for example, "I need to make a phone call first," "When I get back from walking the dog," "When I finish reading this chapter," and so on. This helps children learn they are part of a family unit and their parents' activities are important too.

Electronic Gratification

Recently a seventeen-year-old senior drove herself to a therapy appointment with me. She sent me a text two minutes before the hour to tell me she was there and then knocked on the door at the top of the hour because I didn't respond. This happens frequently. This is a great therapeutic opportunity for me to talk about waiting and social norms, but it is also indicative of how often she does this with other people.

—Dr. Ron

To complicate things even further, children have developed a very low frustration tolerance for waiting, thanks to technology. With the introduction of new devices that provide information at the touch of a finger, such as tablet computers, there is not much for which children and teens are required to "wait." Not only do they have access to any television show on demand, pictures via digital cameras (rather than waiting for film to be developed or prints made), and directions via GPS (rather than using a paper map), but they also have access to answers to questions within seconds of asking, thanks to the Internet. The convenience that accompanies smartphones has strengthened the need for instant gratification even more, as we discuss further in chapter 7. This need for immediate response is encouraged throughout most aspects of their lives. Teens today often communicate with their parents and friends via text messaging. In fact, it has quickly become the primary form of communication for many. It is rare to find a teen without a cell phone within reach at all times. Therefore, if they receive a text message from a friend, it is expected that they will respond right away, which is the social norm. If they want to ask about plans for the day or what happened during a party, they will get the information within seconds of texting the question to a friend. There is no delay in finding out the information. Now let's look at some examples parents have shared with us of the low frustration tolerance of their kids.

- When my child is waiting to be picked up and I'm not there right away, he doesn't wait long before he calls or texts me asking where I am.
- My children don't have to wait through commercials or even wait for the day a show is broadcast because they watch TV shows on demand.

- My family takes advantage of online shopping and prefers products that can be shipped overnight.
- My child passes time spent waiting in lines or for an appointment with electronic entertainment, such as playing a mobile phone game.
- If there is a problem at school, my child will immediately call me for solutions or assistance.
- My family doesn't need a road map because we have a GPS device, and my children understand that if they get lost, they can call someone right away rather than use logic and reasoning to figure out what to do.

There is no stopping the trend of convenience. However, there are many ways to encourage and support patience and delayed gratification. The following are some examples:

- Talk with your children about what to do if you are not there to pick them up at the expected time.
- Have children participate in planning family activities, including creating a schedule and identifying the items or equipment that are needed for that activity. This demonstrates that fun activities don't just happen but require forethought and careful planning.
- If a child wants something, such as a new game on his Nintendo DS, a toy, or expensive item of clothing, ask the child to help out with some household responsibilities first. This is not for allowance or so that he can get the game; it is to communicate that parents and kids help each other.
- Determine times when electronics are not allowed, such as dinner, family time, after 8:00 p.m., and so on.

- If a child wants to do something, discuss a plan to do it later in the week rather than that day.

Electronics play a significant role for most of us on a daily basis. When used reasonably, these gadgets can add a lot of convenience and joy to our lives. For some people, however, electronics condition them to need instant feedback, which simply cannot be sustained in a healthy manner. We have offered some suggestions to help you manage the benefits and consequences of technology.

Teach the Lessons Early

At what age is it appropriate to begin to teach self-discipline through delayed gratification? Infants depend on care providers to meet their needs immediately. If they are hungry, they should be fed; if they are wet, they should be changed; if they have gas, they should be burped. As infants develop into toddlers, their "needs" expand into "wants," and then the bait-and-switch technique becomes a parent's go-to survival response. If a toddler wants to play with your keys but you need to drive the car, you distract the child with another toy and sneak the keys away.

The challenge for many parents is in knowing when children are ready to learn they cannot have everything they want when they want it. It is the shift from instant gratification to delayed gratification. If a two-year-old child says, "Milk," it is important to encourage him to continue to use words to communicate, so quickly getting him milk is exactly what a parent does. But if a six-year-old or a twelve-year-old child says, "I want milk," he is very capable of waiting. Similarly, if your two-year-old child is absolutely taken with a toy at your neighbor's house, you may go out the next day to buy the toy for your child. However, if you do that for your four-year-old or ten-year-old child, you are encouraging the expectation for instant gratification.

When parents provide things for their children immediately, it denies children the opportunity to learn how to meet their needs on their own. They never develop the skills or comfort to care for themselves. In addition, it is not realistic for people to expect all things to come quickly just because they want them right away. Therefore, developing this expectation in children can only lead to dissatisfaction.

Even Toddlers Can Learn to Wait

Children as young as nine months old can begin to learn the lesson of waiting. The younger the child, the more fun the waiting should be, but the lesson is the same. The following games can teach young children how to take turns and gain patience.

Nine to Twelve Months
Play a game, for example, by dropping blocks in a toy, making sounds, or rolling a ball back and forth. Before you take your turn each time, say, "One, two, three...," and then wait two to three seconds with an expectant look to keep the baby engaged, and then take your turn.

Twelve to Eighteen Months
Play the same game described for the younger baby but extend the wait time to five seconds.

Eighteen Months to Two and a Half Years

When your child wants something, you can introduce the verbal request to wait, but the waiting time will be very short. For example, if your child reaches up and says, "Up," you can say, "OK, wait for two seconds" then count to two and pick your child up.

Three Years and Older

As children get older, the verbal expectation for them to wait can be more direct. For example, you may say to a three-and-a-half-year-old child, "OK, let's wait and count to ten" or "OK, I can do that when I put these three groceries away." Kids can very quickly grow wary of the phrase "in a minute," so it is best to choose another way to show them the time to wait.

There will be times when you won't be able to use these strategies. If you have a screaming toddler who has not had a nap, it would not be a good time to practice waiting. That is OK. Introduce these as games and when the child is in a playful mood. Then when you really need him to wait, he will be more comfortable doing so.

The Pressure Trap

Parents feel proud sharing their children's accomplishments. They also worry about their children and are more confident if they feel they are ahead of the competition. This makes parents vulnerable to pushing them too fast.

In today's culture of raising children, there is a lot of pressure to provide children every advantage to get ahead. Parents are concerned that if they don't, their children will be left behind academically, developmentally, athletically, or socially. Parents work to help their children to be at the top of the class, to be the best player on a team, and to have the most friends. Parents want their children to feel confident and good about themselves, so they encourage extra enrichment to push them ahead. For example, if they are not at the top levels, children receive tutoring to move them higher in the class, and young athletes receive individual coaching to become the best player on the team. Parents may even plan elaborate events such as expensive birthday parties so that kids will want to be their children's friends. But what if these expectations do not fit with the abilities, desires, or personality of the child? The expectation to excel at everything often pushes children to perform past their typical developmental capability in at least some areas, because no child can be in the top levels of everything. The result is that very often the child is not going to be able to meet her parents' expectations. This can lead to disappointment on the part of the parents and feelings of failure on the part of the child.

It is typically not the parents' intention to communicate to their children that they need to be the best at everything, but look how it happens so easily:

Mary is a good student (B+/A−), has played piano for five years, and is the catcher for the softball team. When she brings home a report card or test, her parents talk with her about her grade and how she can pull her B+ up to an A. One weekend, there is a piano recital and her parents point out that there is a boy three years younger who is playing a more difficult piece, more out of amazement at his skill, not trying to make Mary feel bad. Then, at her next soft-ball game, she makes two errors at the plate, resulting in the other team earning two runs. Her coach talks to her about some extra catching practice the following week.

—Dr. Darlene and Dr. Ron

Often children and teens talk with us about the pressure they feel from the different adults in their lives. It is an alluring trap for parents to push their children ahead and "give" their children all the advantages. Their intention is to help their children to be their best. While they want to offer their children support, the message is interpreted as "You are not good enough, and you need to be better." We see a clear relationship between the pressure that parents put onto their children and the pressure they must feel to be perfect parents themselves.

The Pressure Parents Feel

Parents feel pressure from very early on to provide their children with all the early advantages. Whether it is the push to teach their child to read as a toddler or begin music lessons before they can walk, they hear about all the new and innovative programs that other parents are introducing to their children and begin to question whether they are doing all they can for their own children. This begins the pattern of questioning their parenting philosophies. What may have begun as, "I just want my child to be happy," "I want them to develop their own interests," or "Everyone has different strengths," turns into, "I should be looking at preschools now," "I should find an early foreign language class," and "Now that my child is three years old, we need to start music lessons."

Raising children is a huge responsibility that requires parents to be considerate of many decisions they make on their child's behalf. In so many instances, parents question their decisions or their child's ability compared to what other children are doing. This is the parent pressure trap. This parent trap is even more alluring when what the other children are doing is seen as more advanced or prestigious. For example, there are many assumptions made about the child who attends an academically based preschool rather than a play-based preschool, a child who plays on a "club" or competitive sports team rather than a recreational team, or a student who takes honors classes rather than general classes. Even if the child is not doing well in one of those programs, it is assumed the child is better or more gifted than his or her peers. Parents of children at all ages feel this pressure, and it entices them to fall into the trap of pushing their children to move ahead.

It is important for parents to understand that this is pressure *they* feel, not the child. Children want to hang out, have fun, and do activities of their choosing. Most children aren't thinking about which programs are more enriching.

Because no parent has all the answers, there is a constant question of whether she is doing the right thing for her kids. It is natural for parents to compare themselves to others. If they admire something another parent is doing, they want to emulate that. Parents often work for their perception of the "ideal," but they can lose sight of whether it is ideal for their child. It is so easy to fall into the pressure trap without even realizing it.

There Is No Such Thing as a Perfect Parent

The pressure trap is really about parents wanting to do everything in their power to help their children be successful and happy. What is often overlooked is the idea that in many ways, our children's success and happiness are developed out of a sense of confidence and pride. These skills are not acquired because of early immersion in language or music but rather by a child finding a passion and being supported to follow it.

Remember that no two kids are the same. Just because some program or support worked for one child does not mean it will be as effective for others.

Try not to overmanage or overschedule your child's daily routines. Every child has a unique potential, and maintaining a healthy balance between providing opportunities and preventing burnout is one of a parent's biggest responsibilities.

The Giving Trap

Parents don't want their children to feel left out. The result is that parents fall into the trap of giving material items to their kids that they didn't have to work for.

We constantly marvel at the number of kids with whom we interact who have new and expensive smartphones, tablets, and music devices. Often, these devices were not received as presents for a birthday or holiday but are things that are just given to kids.

When asked, some parents will say, "He said the old phone didn't allow him to do the things his friends do. He needed to have the smartphone." Other parents enjoy the glee they see in their children when they give them something so cool.

Whether it is designer clothes or the latest technology, we hear from kids every day that their parents need to understand how important it is for them to have certain "cool" things or else their peers will tease them and they'll feel left out. Parents think that if they can fix the problem (i.e., by buying their children whatever they've asked for), then their children will be accepted. A lot of parents will tell us that they know that it is probably better if their kids work for these things, but the pull is strong and it is difficult not to give in. As a result, parents get caught in the giving trap.

In past generations, children learned to work hard in order to achieve goals. They had a choice: they could do the work now and get what they wanted later or else *not* do the work and *not* get what they wanted. The situation was very simple. Back then, gifts were considered extra special, not an expected item. Instead, teens would get a job to earn money to pay for things they wanted. Very often, this is not the case for this generation.

Parents tell us they want their children to have what they never had or that they want to raise their children differently because they felt deprived when they were growing up. The result is often that parents overindulge their children. Think about the increase in material things that children are given in this generation. How many children pay the monthly bill for their phones or for the apps they download to their electronic devices? We hear more and more about children who get an allowance every week but don't have to do anything to earn it. To keep teens from feeling "different," parents buy them the latest technology, such as smartphones, tablets, and video games. This is not in line with the "you need to work for it" philosophy that most people will agree is so important.

Teach Them How to Earn Their Things

The number of children and teens who are earning money for things they want has dropped significantly. Statistics show that the number of teenagers who work hit an all-time low over the past four years despite the drop in the overall unemployment rate. Kevin Hall reported on the McClatchy DC Washington Bureau that the rate of teens who worked dropped from 52 percent in 1999 to 32.35 percent in 2013.[4] Having a part-time job in high school is a valuable way for teenagers to learn responsibility and independence and the value of earning money, organization, and planning, as well as gain esteem in their ability to work. However, with the substantial increase in overscheduling that we discussed previously, they are often not allotted the time to get a job, which in turn leads to parents paying for extra things rather than teens earning money themselves. This reinforces the lesson that things are easily obtained with little to no work.

There are several ways to teach kids the value of working for things they want. First, allowance should not, as a matter of course, be given freely. Kids need to earn their allowance, and many families use chores as ways for their children to earn money. How allowance is allotted can differ depending on the family's schedule and other factors. For example, some families do well with chore charts that assign specific tasks to certain children. Another option is to provide a specified amount of money for each chore completed. For children to feel a part of the family's responsibilities, there should also be some things that they do without being paid—for example, setting or clearing the dinner table, taking out garbage when asked (unless it is a daily responsibility), and helping out on weekends when needed. On the other hand, there should be things that are outside of daily help that they can do to earn money, such as doing laundry or yard work, washing a car, or doing extra cleaning (vacuuming, dusting, or scrubbing).

Another way to teach kids the value of working for things they want is encouraging a job outside the home. Some students are able to work a part-time job, while others are able to have intermittent jobs, such as babysitting or dog walking. Jobs are different from chores because they allow teenagers to manage the responsibilities on their own and allow them to gain confidence and pride in earning money for work they did well.

Have Them Work for It

Introducing the concept of earning money to buy something is great on many levels. Not only does it teach children delayed gratification and that things are earned and not given, but it also teaches them how to plan and work toward achieving a goal. If you have children who become angry when you tell them they can't have something, this approach does not give them a refusal but options to get what they want. It lets them know you are listening to what is important to them and provides the message that all goals are attainable. They just need to take the initiative to obtain the goals themselves.

When a child asks for something that costs money, it is great to be supportive. That does not mean buying the item for the child; it is simply sharing the child's interest in something new. Then parents can help their children think of ways to pay for it.

- "If you help me clean up the yard today, you will earn that toy you asked for."
- "Yes, that video game at Sue's was really cool. I agree it would be fun for you guys to play it together. Let's find out how much it is and talk about how you can pay for it."
- "Yeah. I am loving that new style of jeans. They are much more than I would normally pay for your jeans. I can give you the money that I would normally set aside for your jeans, and then we can talk about how you can earn any extra that you need."

For expensive items, finding out how much work it takes to earn enough money teaches understanding of the value of a dollar. This process teaches delayed gratification, problem solving, and planning, which are the exact skills parents strive to teach.

- "You're right. That is a really cool phone. How much is it? Let's find out when the contract on your phone is up and what credit you can get toward a new phone. If you want it sooner, I can help you find ways to earn the money."
- "You want your own car when you are sixteen? Let's determine the cost of different types of cars and you can decide how much you need to work to earn the money to buy one."

The Guilt Trap

Parents don't want to be the reason for their child's unhappiness. When parents believe they are the reason their child is upset, they are more likely to feel guilty and fall into the trap of giving in without their children doing their part.

Most children attempt to goad their parents into doing things for them. This is developmentally typical and normal, and often, these attempts work. A child may ask in a very sweet way, "Mom, please, please, please. Can you get me that doll?" A child may wear their parents down with repetitive requests or tantrums when they don't get a positive response the first time. Or a child may use a plea that provokes feelings of guilt from the parent, such as, "I really want to get a good grade in that class, but if you don't bring me the paper and I turn it in late, it will be impossible." The table quickly turns, making the parent responsible for providing the solution. Fixing the problem alleviates the guilt and makes peace with the child, but is it ever really just once?

Parents often question their decisions because they feel guilty about causing their child's unhappiness. When parents set limits, they risk their child being angry at them. It can cause arguments in the home and their child telling them, "I hate you," "You don't understand," or "You ruined my life." While this is developmentally typical, what parent wants to invite this negativity into the home? Thus parents fall into the trap of giving in to their child's demands, which might seem to solve the problem in the short term but has long-term consequences.

Sometimes Busy Parents Try to Fill the Void

There's no doubt about it: today's parents are extremely busy. There are also more families with two parents working full-time. A very common phenomenon that we see is parents give in to their children because they feel guilty about not being more available. Parents communicate to us that they feel guilty about not being there during the day for school activities, playdates, and the like. Therefore, they are more likely to rescue their children or provide them with expensive material things when they haven't really earned the privilege. It could be as simple as making a specific meal because their child tells (not asks) them to, or it could be buying them the latest technological gadget.

Busy parents may also be more likely to provide their children answers to problems or dilemmas right away rather than assisting them in learning how to solve the problem on their own because it feels good to provide comfort and see the relief on the child's face. Consider the child who says, "Mom, I didn't like what you packed me for lunch, so I didn't eat it and now I am really hungry. We need to stop and get food on the way home." For many of us, this touches the guilt button. *My child skipped lunch and now doesn't feel good because I didn't pack food she likes.* To ease the child's discomfort and the parent's guilt, it would be easy to stop and get food on the way home. However, this response supports instant gratification and makes it the parent's problem. Another response is to say, "You can make yourself something to eat when we get home. If you would like other food in your lunch, come talk to me about it and we can choose some different things." This response teaches the child to take responsibility for self-care (sometimes you have to eat things you don't love because they are good for you and your body needs it), independence (making his or her own snack), and planning (for future lunches).

Establish a "Fun Friday"

Working parents have it tough because when they are not working, they are maintaining all the household responsibilities. There is not a lot of free time. Therefore, if their child asks them to do something extra such as play a game or set up a playdate, a common answer is, "Not today," with no set plans for doing it in the future. This can prompt even more guilt, especially when the result is more TV or more electronics to keep children busy while parents get things done.

Try to establish in your routine a "Fun Friday." Friday tends to work best for this, but any day works great—just choose a day that neither the parent nor child has to fulfill responsibilities. That means no laundry, house-cleaning, homework, or any other things that fill up free time. Now when your child asks you to play a game with her, you can say, "That sounds great. Let's plan that for Fun Friday." If a child wants to have friends over, you can say, "That would be a great Fun Friday thing to do." This way the child knows that it will happen and the parent can feel excited about the plan rather than guilty. This can also be a fun parent day. No responsibilities? Who doesn't want that for a day?

Identify and Avoid Parent Traps

Remember, it is a child's job to test limits and find ways to meet his or her desires. It is the job of parents and educators to set the limits and guide children with responsible ways to achieve their wishes. Now that you know what the traps are, the next step is identifying when you fall in them. It is important for parents to know when there is a risk of giving rather than teaching. Here are some questions to ask yourself to find out if you have fallen into a parenting trap:

1. Does your child tell you about a problem with no thoughts of a solution?
2. Are you a problem solver and find it difficult to listen without giving a solution?
3. Does your child get angry or upset if you don't fix a problem?
4. Does your child make you feel guilty if you don't do something for him or her?
5. Do your children use their friends' parents as comparisons in conversations with you?
6. Do you find that your children have everything they want long before a birthday or holiday?
7. Do you find yourself going overboard with a birthday party because you have seen other parents do it?
8. Do you find yourself writing letters trying to pick your child's teacher every year?
9. Do you find yourself doing too much of your children's school projects for them?
10. Do you stop whatever you are doing to respond to your child's request?
11. Do you catch yourself rescuing your child and tell yourself it is just this one time?
12. Do you interrupt an activity or meeting to answer your child's text even if it is not an emergency?

Once the trap or traps are identified, the next step is to avoid them and be prepared for what comes next. You know your child is not going to be happy about being told no or having to work hard to fix a problem on his own. When a child brings you a problem, remember, your child is likely feeling very anxious about it. Your child is looking to ease that anxiety. Instead of fixing the problem, your role is to provide gentle guidance and allow your child to consider possible solutions on his own.

Avoid Parenting Traps and Support Your Child

- When your child approaches you with a complaint or problem, your first response should always be "Tell me what is going on." This communicates that you are listening and interested in what he or she has to say.
- Next, ask, "What solutions have you thought about so far?" or "What is your plan?" This prompts your child to begin thinking about how to solve the problem. This also shows that you are still listening. Even though it is very tempting to provide solutions at this point, refrain from doing so.
- Let your child know that it's OK if she can't find a solution right away. In fact, learning to face a problem and remain calm is very important in problem solving.
- After your child has identified some possible solutions, invite him to consider the consequences or possible outcomes by asking, "What do you think would happen if you did that?" or "How do you think they will react if you do that?"

- Only after a long discussion and a lot of listening should you ask questions such as, "Did you consider…?" or "Would you like help thinking of some other options?"

In this chapter we identified five significant traps that often impact parenting. After introducing the traps, we provided age-appropriate suggestions for self-awareness and parenting behaviors. In the following chapters you will see these traps again, but in the context of various common situations that parents routinely face.

CHAPTER 2
Missed Opportunities When Parents Rescue Their Children

Every year our children are asked to participate in a fund-raiser at school. To entice the kids to sell more merchandise the school offers incentives like, "If you sell ten magazines you can attend a pizza party on Friday," or "If you sell twenty rolls of wrapping paper you will get to play video games in the Game Truck after lunch next week." We routinely hear from parents that they don't want their children to miss out on the pizza party or the video games because they want to go and all of their friends are going. This quickly evolves into parents being more invested in their child meeting the goal. They remind them often to go talk to neighbors or call family members. Yet if the child doesn't follow through, the parents jump in to rescue their child from feeling disappointed about a missed reward— for example, by asking their friends and coworkers to buy merchandise if their child didn't sell enough. In this way, the child will be rewarded for minimal independent effort.
—Dr. Darlene and Dr. Ron

One of the most common mistakes that parents make is failing to recognize the difference between supporting their children and rescuing them. When a parent rescues his children from a conflict, he is "doing" it for them. In the previous chapter, we identified this as the rescue trap. By contrast, when parents support their child in solving the problem independently, parents are "encouraging" the process of critical thinking and tolerance. The child is using problem-solving, planning, and social skills while at the same time learning to tolerate the discomfort that comes from not feeling sure about the resolution. This process is essential practice for developing children and teenagers, and it is lost when they are rescued.

Anxiety as a Healthy Emotion

Anxiety is a state of uneasiness and apprehension about future uncertainties. In other words, anxiety occurs when a person does not know what will happen. Parents know that life is full of uncertainty. We cannot change that for ourselves or for our children. What we can do is prepare our children for how to deal calmly with life's uncertainties.

> *One week, I received calls from three separate families wanting therapy for a child who was feeling anxious and beginning to avoid activities. One wanted to stay home from school because she was afraid to talk to her teacher about missing an assignment; one wanted to come home from school because he was nervous about talking to longtime friends at lunch after a misunderstanding the day before; and one wanted to quit soccer and avoid practice because she didn't think the other players thought she was good enough.*
>
> —Dr. Darlene

Many teens come into our office because they are feeling anxious, and they cope with this feeling by using avoidance tactics. The causes of anxiety among teens vary, but the overarching theme is that teens have had very little experience facing challenges without a parent to rescue them. Time and time again, we hear about teens who have expressed anxiety to their parents, only for their parents to ease their discomfort by solving the problem for them. In doing so, teens fail to realize that anxiety is temporary and that resolving the problem on their own could actually decrease their anxiety. Instead, they learn a false sense of security that everything will work out, because their moms or dads will always be there to save them. Teenagers who have never had the opportunity to practice problem solving on their own are at a huge disadvantage when they make a teenage-sized mistake that their parents can't protect them from. For example, we often have parents share with us that they can't believe their teenager was pulled over by the police for being out after curfew or being caught with friends who were drinking. These same teenagers were driven to school every day, their only social activities were organized by adults, and they were so busy there was no time for chores or family responsibilities. Their parents then expect them to make good choices when they had no chance for practice in doing so before. We know it is difficult to let children have the freedom to mess some things up, but allowing it when they are younger prepares them for the choices they will need to make later on.

A parent's motivation for attempting to rescue their child typically stems from the parent's own anxiety and a sense of protectiveness. We all want to prevent our children from having a negative experience, especially when we have the power or knowledge to fix it. Yet one of the best gifts you can give your children is teaching them not to fear uncertainty. Your children will gain self-confidence in knowing they have the ability to deal with whatever circumstance comes their way. It can be as simple as letting your child go to the restroom by himself in a familiar restaurant. It's possible that he might get lost on the way back to the table, so he may feel anxious. But after walking around looking for you, or even asking a staff member for directions, he will probably make it back to the table with the realization that he has the power to solve his own problems. Another option is to give your children two or three items to retrieve for you at a familiar grocery store on their own. This type of solo experience increases children's self-confidence, pride, and sense of responsibility. While some parents may feel wary about this level of independence and might think, "What if he gets lost?" we say, "In this safe environment, I hope he gets lost so he can figure out what to do."

Watch from Afar

If you are feeling anxious about letting your child experience a new situation, you can always monitor from a distance. Watch from across the room as your child navigates his way to the restroom, or let him walk the last two blocks to school alone (you can even monitor from your car), or sit across the park as he plays with the other children. But remember, watch from afar and don't meddle in the challenges that may arise. If your child gets lost, watch and see how he figures out how to find you before you step in. This requires patience, but as you watch your child figure out what to do, maybe you will also develop more confidence in him. Even though it is difficult, as long as the child is safe, don't jump in to help.

The Different Ways Parents Rescue Children

When parents rescue their children, they prevent their children from figuring out how to solve problems. Problem solving takes practice, and the best practice comes from opportunities they encounter in daily life. From infancy to preschool to middle school and beyond, each of these stages poses new challenges for children and parents alike. With each challenge, children face new and often uncomfortable situations, and there is the temptation for parents to rescue them.

The Skill Rescue

The "skill rescue" can begin at a very young age and happens when parents jump in to do a task for their children rather than allowing them to struggle through it until they learn how. When you see your toddler struggling to put on a shoe, it may be tempting to do it for her, particularly when you are in a hurry or late for an appointment. This can then extend to the preschool child who didn't finish the art project—perhaps you just need to add that last finishing touch. This is how the pattern of rescuing children begins.

Before children even begin school, they have many natural opportunities for developing confidence in trying to do new things. As infants, children learn self-help skills (such as feeding themselves). As toddlers, they learn to dress themselves and how to wash their hands, as well as social skills (making eye contact, sharing, maintaining two-way conversations) and problem-solving skills (pretend play, puzzles, exploration) on a daily basis. These are opportunities for them to learn through the natural environment. Jean Piaget, a leading theorist on human development, describes children at this age as "little scientists," actively exploring and trying to make sense of their environment.[1] At about third or fourth grade, a child's responsibilities begin to change and his school schedule becomes more structured. Because of these changes, the opportunity for natural skill building decreases. The challenges also become more difficult, and the pressure to rescue your child grows stronger. Therefore, take advantage of these early opportunities that, to children, come naturally.

One reason we wrote this book is because we recognized these temptations and realized we too constantly have to check ourselves. Watching your child struggle in any way is hard (when it is not amusing). The temptation is so strong to stop the struggle, but we also realize that, in doing so, we prevent our children from developing skills that are going to be essential as they grow up. One way to monitor your impulse to rescue your children is to make a rule to observe them for five to ten seconds before deciding whether to help. And remember, every time you see your children being challenged, stand back and recognize that it is a learning opportunity that will teach essential skills that they will use throughout life.

Replace Missed Opportunities

Families are busy, and there are times when waiting for a toddler to dress herself, a child to make her own lunch, or a teen to finish his laundry is not an option because the family is late and has somewhere to be. These things happen sometimes, and it's OK. Parents just need to be aware of missed opportunities so they can practice these skills at another time and provide new opportunities for their children to develop.

For example, in a family of four, mornings may be chaotic. Bobby, a toddler, rarely has the opportunity to dress himself. To create a new opportunity to learn this skill, Bobby's parents allow him to dress for bed at night or on weekends.

The Social Rescue

We can all agree that we want our children to have healthy friendships and be well liked by their peers. Parents remember the ups and downs of their own friendships when they were children. They also remember how much it hurt when they did not feel socially accepted. Therefore, it is very easy for them to empathize with their children as they experience the same trials and tribulations of confusing social dynamics and want to protect them.

Some lucky kids are born socially gifted, and the art of making friends comes naturally to them with almost no effort. Most kids are in a different category and have to work at least a little to make friends. Learning how to interact with people is a skill that can be learned and practiced. However, often children don't get the opportunity to practice these skills without parental interference. The social rescue occurs when well-intentioned parents impact the opportunity for their children to practice and to work things out for themselves.

A parent of a high school student shared with me that she had heard that her son's friends were making fun of him for his choice of girlfriend. The boy was pretty broken up about his loyalties and torn between his friends and his girlfriend. By all accounts, the girl in question was smart, sweet, attractive, and from a great family. The parent was so concerned that she called the parents of the other boys to ask them to have their children apologize for making her son so uncomfortable and to stop their teasing. She also wanted the fellow parents, and me, to keep this secret so her son wouldn't be even more upset.

—Dr. Ron

In the previous example, the boy needed to deal with a fairly common social issue (teasing), but instead of solving the problem himself, his mother did it for him. His approach may not have been the same as his parent's and it may not have resulted in the outcome he wanted, but that is OK. As we stated previously in this chapter, kids learn the best through practice. With practice comes the opportunity to learn problem-solving skills and build self-esteem. By dealing with social dilemmas on their own, children and teens learn they can deal with a problem independently when one arises in the future.

Support Opportunities to Practice Social Skills

Children need the opportunity to practice social skills. Yet some kids don't know how to make those opportunities for themselves. Parents can help with this. What follows are some age-based interventions that can help children socially and promote independence.

- **Preschool:** Parents of preschool children need to be the ones to plan the playdates and group activities. The more the merrier, but make sure your children have some downtime in their schedule too. Give your children some options of activities available to them (art activity, backyard play, go to the park, etc.). Several options can be made available, and your children can choose if they want to do one of them, none of them, or morph them together in some creative way.

- **Elementary school:** When your children are at this age, you can help them set up playdates on their own by providing them with parameters. For example, you can say, "This week you can have a friend over Monday or Thursday after school until five o'clock." Have healthy but popular snacks on hand and fun games to play and offer to pick up the kids and drive them home. It's fine to help get the kids to your house, but then give them some space to practice social skills and play on their own. You know your children best, so if making conversation causes a lot of anxiety, your children may do better with something structured to start the playdate—for example, inviting a friend to a movie or over to play the new video game.

- **Middle and high school:** When your children are at this age, you should be paying attention to their social issues. A good way to stay involved is to ask questions. For example, if it seems like your child is struggling to make friends, ask her about things she has done to be more connected to her peers. Sometimes giving your child an opportunity to talk things out with you is enough, while other times your child may need a little more support. Resist the temptation to "fix" things, but feel free to help. If your child is reluctant to call a friend to hang out, it can help to provide your child with something specific to call about (e.g., going to the football game together, going to a movie, or checking out a viral YouTube video). In this generation, text messaging can be really helpful for kids who are nervous picking up the phone and making a call. Texting can be a great way for them to develop comfort with organizing activities. After a couple of times communicating through text, encourage them to call those friends directly and practice direct communication so that they don't become reliant on texting.

The Academic Rescue

The academic rescue occurs when parents work harder than their children for good grades. It starts in elementary school with micromanaging their children's projects and assignments and continues all the way to high school, where some parents actually do their child's work for him or her. One reason for this is because some adults simply place more value on grades than many children do. Parents see grades as the key to better teachers, higher self-esteem, honors classes in high school, and ultimately, acceptance at a great college. While these things may be true, if the parent is the one earning the grade, then honors classes and an Ivy League school may not be in their child's best interest. If you find yourself getting overinvolved in your child's schoolwork, ask yourself how much of your motivation is to protect the all-important grade.

With the Instant Gratification Generation, the academic rescue is made even easier with the introduction of the cell phone. With the touch of a button, moms or dads are available at all times to save the day and kids come to expect it. If children don't think they have to solve their own problems, they will defer to a parent every time, and texting makes it even easier. Children and teens don't need to wait and think of the possible options available to them. Instead, they can reach their parents on their cell phone and get the solution instantly. The following are real examples from parents who have shared their experiences with us.

- "Mom, I forgot my paper. It is due today. Can you bring it to the school?"
- "Dad, I need you to bring me my track shoes for practice after school."
- "Mom, my shorts don't meet dress code. Can you bring me new ones because they are going to make me wear my PE clothes?"
- "Dad, I need to finish an art project, and I need to have paints, poster board, and glue. It is due tomorrow."

People process information more fully if it is meaningful to them. Think about every time you ask your child to pick his towel off the floor after a shower. If every time you see the towel on the floor you say, "You need to hang up the towel," and then put it on the hook yourself, your child is not likely to ever do it. He probably isn't avoiding the task out of disrespect but because he doesn't remember to do it. Now what if you said he could not have a playdate, go out with friends, or play with his favorite electronics every time he left a towel on the floor? Next time, he will pick it up because by communicating the consequences (and following through), you have made the request more meaningful and memorable to him. Experiences are much more memorable than words. When your child forgets to fulfill a responsibility (to turn in homework, bring in money for a field trip, wash PE clothes, let you know about something he needs for an activity, etc.), allowing your child to experience the consequences will make a stronger impact.

> *There was a fifth-grade field trip for an overnight stay on an aircraft carrier, but the spaces were limited and it was first come, first served. A mother shared that she gave her daughter the paperwork to turn in and that it was her responsibility to set her alarm and be ready to go to school early if she really wanted to go on the field trip. If she forgot or didn't get herself up early, she could turn it in when she wanted but would need to experience the chance there were no spaces left.*
>
> —Dr. Ron

Putting It All Together

The Issue

Parents hate seeing their children upset or anxious. They want to do everything they can to prevent them from having a negative experience.

The Trap

Parents have the ability to solve many of their children's problems easily and quickly. This solves the problems with fewer tears, arguments, and possibly a more positive outcome. But remember, this deprives them of essential practice.

The Alternative

Resist the temptation to rescue children and teens. Allow them to come up with the solutions to resolve problems.

1. Make waiting the rule, not the exception. Begin this expectation when they are young. When your toddler, child, or teen makes a request, take your time in responding to the request. Adjust the wait time depending on the age of the child.
2. Find regular opportunities for your children to do things on their own without your assistance.
3. Allow children to grapple with finding the solutions to problems. Be available as a sounding board, but don't jump in to offer the easy answer. And don't rework their solution if it is not perfect. It probably won't be, and that's OK.
4. Let children take chances. As long as personal safety isn't involved, one of the best ways to learn about problem solving is to get experience doing it.
5. Ask questions after the fact. Feel free to go over what happened and ask what they might do differently next time.

6. Allow children to experience natural consequences to their actions and choices. Experiencing the consequences will be memorable and is what will encourage them to do it differently the next time.

CHAPTER 3
Make No Mistake about It
Everyone Makes Mistakes

I will never forget the third session I had with a mother of a two-year-old toddler. She and her husband sought help with coparenting their daughter. On the third session, her husband was late, and I had thirty minutes with her alone. She was following a week of minimal sleep (her daughter was still not sleeping through the night) and she was feeling very fragile. Five minutes into the session, she disclosed that there were times when she wanted to get in her car and drive to a faraway location without her cell phone. She then looked up mortified that she shared this secret. When I shared with her that this is a common thought among parents, she went on to describe a significant period of postpartum depression that she never told anyone about. She said it was a time that she was supposed to cherish with her daughter and that she must have been doing something wrong because she did not feel the "bliss" that every one of her friends described. After the first year, her feelings of depression went away, but she was

plagued with guilt. She shared that she has felt so guilty about wanting time away from her daughter that she began to overcompensate with setting very few limits for her daughter—the reason for the disagreements with her husband. She was then laden with the guilt of not setting limits for her daughter.

—Dr. Darlene

The Pressure to Be Perfect

Boom. The minute you become a parent, the pressure is on. For perhaps the first time in your life, you feel that now you need to do everything right. The fear of making a mistake has never been so prominent. When you know that you are going to become a parent, you feel the pressure to follow the recommendations and advice of all your friends, family, and even the strangers at the grocery store. We call this the beginning of the pressure trap. They must know more than you, right? If you're not taking advantage of every bit of advice, you must not be doing everything you can for your baby. The race to do it right begins.

For many parents, this type of thinking occurs as soon as they find out they will be having a baby. You begin to look at the events around you with a new outlook. Not only are you more aware of the families you see at every restaurant, grocery store, or social event, but you're also more attentive to the onslaught of commercials and media that target new parents. You also become inundated with the anecdotes, stories, and advice from most of the people you encounter. You may think you are simply attending a friend's birthday dinner, but once people hear (or see) that you are having a baby, you hear opinions ranging from neonatal care to raising a teenager: "You should sign up your baby for preschool now; otherwise, she won't get into one that will have her reading before elementary school." Then there is the never-ending literature. Beginning with pregnancy, there are thousands of books telling you the perfect diet while pregnant, books to read to the baby in utero, ways to reduce stress to make a more calming experience for the developing fetus, how to foster a love of music in a growing fetus, and so on, and so on. How does a person keep up?

It seems like everyone else has it figured out. For this reason, many new parents don't feel comfortable sharing their concerns or mistakes with other people as they are navigating the world of sleepless nights, frustration, and feelings of helplessness. They fear that if they did, other parents would see them as incompetent. Or even worse, it would be admitting they might actually *be* incompetent. Instead, parents focus on the available literature and media outlets for parenting information. Unfortunately, while those resources offer many useful ideas, they don't often include the important section that says, "Mistakes will happen and that is OK" or the section that says, "If you skip a day following the advice of this book because you are busy, on vacation, or just plain tired, no worries, you can start again the next day." Yet that is real life. Mistakes will happen, and that is OK.

Embracing the challenges of parenting allows a more open and honest disclosure of the trials and tribulations that accompany parenting. When parents are lucky enough to have a group of peers who are comfortable sharing their insecurities, it takes away the expectation that everything has to be perfect. One of my most comforting moments happened when I dropped off my son at preschool and a mom greeted me with a laugh and said, "Don't get too close. It was such a crazy morning I forgot to brush my teeth." What a relief to know other parents rush around forgetting basic things too. She is now one of my closest friends.

—Dr. Darlene

Remind yourself that all parents have misgivings. Find someone you can talk to, and you will see that most parents are feeling the same way. Being open with your concerns, and hearing about the concerns of others, provides a sense of normalcy, not guilt. Personally, we think talking about parenting mistakes and mishaps is even better when using a good sense of humor.

A Parent's Desire to Be Perfect Impacts the Kids

The drive to do things right all the time can foster insecurity and guilt in parents, but it also impacts the kids. As clinical psychologists, we have observed over and over the negative impact the message of perfection has on children. First, children learn to feel anxious about making a mistake through the verbal messages of their parents. Very often, this happens because children are privy to adult conversations. Children hear their parents talk about things happening in their own lives. For example, six-year-old Samuel heard his mother talking about his performance in the soccer game, or eight-year-old Emma heard her parents talking about a problem her sister is having with a teacher. They hear their parents' concerns, as well as their complaints. For example, children may hear their parent make casual comments regarding choices for their children such as, "I should have started Alan in baseball when he was four. Now that he is six, he is too far behind," or "I am going to write a letter to make sure Johnny gets Mrs. Brown in second grade because Mrs. Jones really doesn't prepare students for third grade, and I don't want him to be behind." Kids hear and internalize all of this, but they are not developmentally ready to process what they hear. They hear their parent's anxiety about the negative consequences of making the "wrong" choice. They hear that if a mistake is made, all might be lost. Johnny won't be prepared for third grade if he doesn't get Mrs. Brown, and Alan won't ever be a great baseball player because he didn't start when he was four. This can lead to children and adolescents who are reluctant to commit to things or make decisions. What if they make the wrong choice? What if they change their mind? You can see how parents trying to "prepare" their children can send the message that making a mistake should be avoided. No wonder children can be reluctant to make a commitment. Parents may view reluctance as a lack of motivation, but in fact, it may be fear—fear of regret.

A mother of an eight-year-old boy told me she doesn't know what to do because her son tells her he wants to play sports, but when it is time to sign up he changes his mind. Once the season begins, he tells her that he wished he signed up. This is a pattern for the boy. Another parent shared that her daughter often changes her mind about extracurricular activities. She wanted to be in the school play, but the day of sign-ups, she questioned herself and didn't sign up. A few days later, she regretted her decision. She also wanted to be in the school band. All students needed to audition in front of the instructor on a specific day. Again, she questioned herself, did not go, and regretted it soon after. She still mentions feeling bad about not following through. Both students worried about their decision to commit to the activity. They both shared that they didn't know what the "right" thing to do was. This prevented them from trying something new and led to regrets. We frequently encounter these types of situations when working with children and their families.

—Dr. Ron

When children hear their parents worry or question their own choices and decisions, they internalize that anxiety, which impacts their ability to make their own decisions.

Keep Some Things Private

It is important to refrain from including your children in adult discussions about important decisions. A child does not need to hear her parents' negative opinions about her teachers, coaches, friends, and so on. She does not need to hear all the what-if possibilities either. When children hear these discussions, they may learn that it's OK to point out the imperfections of others. It also makes them feel insecure about any imperfections they may have.

Fixing Mistakes, Making Decisions, and Building Confidence

The first step to building confidence in children is allowing them to make mistakes. If you ask most parents or educators, they will tell you, "Of course, it is OK for people to make mistakes. Everyone makes mistakes." That is a wonderful message for children to hear, but we know that children don't always remember or believe what adults say. On the other hand, children remember when the actions of adults are consistent with their words. Children need to see that adults make mistakes and that it is OK when they do so. They then get the gift of watching and learning from those adults. Otherwise, a child thinks that she has to do everything right or she is doomed to failure.

> We all make mistakes. It is important for parents not only to acknowledge our own mistakes to our children but to show them we accept human imperfections and the mistakes of others. This is done through our actions and our words. Acknowledging mistakes with a respectful sense of humor always helps. For example, in our family it is a well-known fact that I am a klutz. In fact, when either one of our boys trips or drops something, they say, "Mom, that was your genetics." We all laugh because it is probably true and we employ a good sense of humor about personal weaknesses. We all have weaknesses. It is also known that I am really organized, good at math, and a great friend. Weaknesses do not define our worth. They are only one very small part of us.
>
> —Dr. Darlene

Telling children it is OK to make mistakes is also meaningless unless the children themselves are allowed to fix them. It is extremely important for children to learn how to solve problems and remedy unexpected outcomes. The only way they can do this is if the adults around them allow them to do so. It is a true challenge for parents to sit back and watch their children fumble their way through a situation without jumping in to help. Often, impatience pushes the adult to step in and solve the problem. Sometimes, even when a child begins to remedy the situation, adults still want to get involved by giving their input to prevent their child from making the wrong decision. However, often, those suggestions are advanced, adult-oriented solutions that are not necessarily appropriate for the child's age or stage of development.

As parents, we want the best outcome for our children, but isn't it better for the child to solve a problem like a child? In fact, most kids would probably be ostracized, or at least get some really funny looks, if they were to talk like an adult and come up with adult-centered solutions. Let's take the following example, which is similar to scenarios we have seen in our practices:

> *Ten-year-old Jimmy comes home upset because his friends did not throw the football to him at recess. Jimmy's mom tells him to let his friends know that it "hurt his feelings" and ask if they would throw it to him more next time. How many times do parents tell their children to let their friends know when their feelings were hurt? As clinical psychologists, we can tell you that it is not developmentally typical for a ten-year-old child to talk like that, and their friends don't usually respond very well to it. Instead of providing solutions, Jimmy's mom can ask him what he can do to make things better, what he might say, what one of his friends would have done, and the like.*

Throughout the first two chapters, we emphasized the importance of giving children opportunities to solve problems on their own. But it's important to keep in mind that when children try to fix a problem independently, they often don't express themselves clearly, they don't approach the problem with confidence, or they don't solve it effectively. As a parent, that can be frustrating. That's OK; it's part of the process. You can't learn calculus before you learn basic math—and even basic math takes practice. Children need to practice problem solving using the basics, and that includes dealing with the mistakes and consequences of their choices.

Children often need support finding a way to fix a mistake. You want to encourage your children to ask for *help* in figuring it out, not ask for solutions. Asking for help is a very responsible way to deal with a problem and should be encouraged. The ability to ask for help when needed is an admirable quality in people of all ages. It shows maturity, strong problem-solving skills, and the ability to be thoughtful.

Asking for help is different than expecting to be given a solution. So when your child approaches you for help, help your child evaluate the options available or encourage your child to approach an issue from another angle. As a parent, it is very rewarding to hear your child think aloud. Try to engage in this process as often as it presents itself.

> *One mother shared that she "celebrates" mistakes. She said that when her children make a mistake, she asks them what they learned from it. If they realize the child made a learning mistake and he comes up with a solution for doing it differently next time, he gets ice cream to celebrate.*
> —Dr. Darlene

Become a Great Listener

When your child comes to you with a problem, don't fall into the trap of providing the solution. It is natural to want to soothe your child's hurt feelings and make things better, but doing so provides only a temporary fix. Your first response should be to listen. As therapists, we often hear children say that they don't talk to their parents about issues because they "won't understand" or "won't listen." Listen well when your child comes to you with a problem. To be a great listener, keep the following skills in mind:

- Don't talk right away. Instead, make attentive eye contact. There will be time for basic questions later.
- Be patient; you can't rush the story.
- Appear interested, such as nodding your head. Put down the phone and remove any distractions.
- Pay attention to what is, and isn't, being said. Your child's body language may give you some clues. Is your child talking quickly, folding his or her arms or looking down, leaving things out of the story, and so on?
- Ask for basic clarification when needed.

When your child is done talking, be supportive. For example, say, "Thanks for sharing. It seems like you have a lot going on right now. Let me know if you think I can do anything to help."

Hovering Parents Impact Decision Making in Children

I ran into a friend at the gym and we began talking about our sons, who are the same age. She said, "He wants to ride his bike here (about four blocks) to the gym by himself for his swimming lesson and I don't want him to." When I asked why not, she said that she didn't know, "something" could happen. When I asked what, she said there was nothing specific. This is a great example of a parent who limits a child because she can't predict or control all the scenarios.

—Dr. Darlene

Great parents tell us all the time that they are afraid to let their children do things on their own. The belief is that the world is a scary place and bad things might happen to them, but if we fail to let our children out of our sight, how can they begin to make decisions by themselves? This phenomenon is known as "hovering," or "helicopter parenting," and it means being unnecessarily overcontrolling or overprotective.[1] Some parents go so far as to clear the way for their children, making sure they don't have to deal with any unexpected or unpleasant challenges; these parents are sometimes called "snowplow parents."[2] This overinvolvement by parents limits problem-solving practice in their children.

Far fewer children walk to and from school by themselves now compared to past generations. It is less common for children to ride their bikes to the local market for a snack, and you rarely see a group of children at a park playing without their parents' supervision. According to the National Center for Safe Routes to School, nearly 50 percent of children walked or rode a bike to school in 1969; today, that number is closer to 13 percent.[3] Modern parents cite traffic and weather concerns, as well as crime, as major barriers to letting their children walk and ride bicycles in the neighborhood. While each parent needs to decide whether her neighborhood is safe for her child, it is important to be aware of the opportunities for development that are missed by children not having these experiences.

Beginning in the toddler years, much of the child's learning is derived from experience. Children learn from the consequences of their actions, both positive and negative. If they don't eat their dinner, they don't get dessert. If they take a toy from another child, they get a time-out. If they are cooperative with their peers, they make friends. Those experiences are a necessary part of early childhood.

As they get older, the opportunities to learn from these types of important experiences should increase—but today's kids aren't being given these chances. Think about the chances to solve problems every day that occurred when children walked home from school without parents. A child's parents want him to learn responsibility by allowing him to walk by himself and be home by an established time. His parents say that if he is late coming home, he will not be allowed to walk home alone again for a month. On the way home, he sees his friends playing a game of tag and wants to join them. Does he keep walking because his parents won't let him walk alone again for a month if he is late? Does he stop and play tag, walk at the same pace, and get home late? Or does he stop and play tag for a few minutes and then run home so he won't be late? This is an opportunity for the child to practice using judgment to make a decision. It also offers him the opportunity to make a mistake by choosing to stay late and losing the privilege of walking home alone for a month. He will learn whether his decision was wise based on the outcome. That outcome will then guide future decisions. Whether it is walking home from school alone, organizing playtime without parents involved, or being responsible for chores without reminders, kids in this generation have fewer opportunities to practice using judgment. When parents are involved in every aspect of their children's lives, children miss these invaluable experiences.

Developmentally, elementary school children are ready to take on responsibility and learn from the positive and negative consequences of their choices. It is very appropriate for children to want increased independence beginning in elementary school, because their brains are ready to practice the decision making that goes along with increased responsibility. By not respecting this or not offering opportunities to practice this need, children are missing an essential opportunity to develop the skills necessary for productive adult lives.

Other Ways for Kids to Be Independent Before and After School

If you do not feel comfortable letting your child walk to school alone, allow your child to play on the playground after school for ten or fifteen minutes before you pick him or her up. Another alternative is to drop your child off a few blocks from school where there are other children and adults walking. Another option is to set a meeting spot for a few kids to meet up and walk together in a group. Better yet, use several of these options. The inconveniences that arise can also be used to teach lessons about planning, decision making, and patience. (Think of the problem solving that is being taught and modeled when someone runs late!) You do not need to do this every day for your child to learn these skills. Once or twice a week works too. If you have a hectic month, pick it up again the month after. Do what works for your family and schedule.

Every situation is different, and each parent will need to decide what is appropriate and safe for his or her child, but it is important to recognize what teaching moments are being missed with the children of this generation. We don't expect that this book will change the culture we live in—after all, the personal safety of our children is of the utmost importance. However, we understand the importance of the opportunities for development that are currently being sacrificed, and we can identify some new ways to fill these gaps. If walking home from school is not an option, then another opportunity to practice independent decision making needs to be identified. To build this independence, your children can do the following activities:

- Bike to a friend's house and call when they get there
- Take money into a restaurant and order and pay for food
- Go ahead of you on hikes or walks
- Prepare his or her own meals and snacks
- Walk the dog alone
- Arrange his or her own playtime or hangouts with friends
- Make his or her own phone calls to organize plans, get homework, or ask questions

How Overscheduling Prevents Skill Development

The parents we encounter every day in our practices are caring, conscientious, and thoughtful. They want to protect their children from negative experiences and to provide all the resources available for them to be happy. These are admirable qualities. The challenge is knowing how much is enough, and how much is too much, particularly as this relates to the child's social life. Most parents know when their kids' schedules are too full, but there is a lot of pressure on parents to make sure their kids don't miss out. As we discussed in the beginning of this chapter, this is part of the pressure trap that compels parents to feel as if they must do everything right. The combination of the pressure to keep kids ahead of the pack and the abundance of programs available makes it so difficult to resist the pull to overschedule them.

We frequently see two consequences to the overscheduled phenomenon. First, children and teens regularly communicate to us that they are stressed out and need time off. They very often say that there are too many activities in their schedule and that they have no time to "just veg out." They tell us that whenever they are trying to relax, their parents ask them about whether they should be doing homework or practicing music or a sport instead. This makes them feel guilty or defensive, which defeats the purpose of having some time off.

The second consequence of being overscheduled is that many kids and teens do not learn how to fill time on their own, so they expect their parents to continuously structure their schedule. If there is a day with some unstructured time, they bombard their parents with questions about what they will do that day. They tend to talk about being bored but have few ideas for how to entertain themselves. Their parents describe the children as needing their attention all the time.

Now, there are some children who do not like to have downtime. They prefer to be busy and keep a full schedule of activities. It wouldn't be a problem if they filled their time themselves; it is the dependence on adults to structure their time for them that is not adaptive. What many parents don't realize is the essential and valuable experiences children get when they have unstructured time to themselves. When adults provide the structure for their schedule, children have no need to make decisions about how to plan their day, solve a problem, manage their time, prioritize activities, and so on. Furthermore, when adults are there to guide their daily activities, it takes away the opportunity for children to make the mistake of poorly managing their time and, therefore, their opportunity to figure out a solution and learn from it. They also learn to tolerate unexpected changes in their plans, which is an invaluable lesson. They may have an idea about what they want to do with that time, but many times it won't go exactly as planned. That requires flexibility, problem solving, and tolerance. When kids are overscheduled, they miss out on those valuable experiences.

As psychologists, we have never worked with a young adult who was struggling because he or she didn't play enough sports, learn enough musical pieces, or speak enough languages. However, we have worked with many who never learned how to tolerate unexpected challenges, develop the confidence to solve problems on their own, or communicate with people they disagree with. Their parents wonder why they are not taking on more responsibility and being more independent. The answer is simple: they never learned how.

Remember the Process, Not Just the Outcome

The trend of child rearing is moving away from a focus on problem solving and, instead, toward an emphasis on the end product or outcome. Today's parents often tell their kids it is OK to make mistakes and then protect them from making them. They also tell their kids that effort is important and that they should try things before making a decision. Yet when parents hear what other kids are doing, they emphasize extracurricular activities their children "should" do and how they "should" perform. Most parents intend to support their children in doing things they enjoy and trying new things, whether or not they are performing at high levels. However, the culture of this generation is to emphasize objective achievement. Therefore, kids hear praise for the strongest reader in the class, the highest grade point averages, or for acceptance to an elite sports team or college.

Statements about objective measures, such as GPA, all-star team membership, reading level, and so on, focus on the end product or the outcome, not the process used to reach the goals, including praise and admiration for independently addressing the mistakes they made along the way. They are also not about the decision making and problem solving that is required to meet the goals. In theory, parents' desires are about the process, but their words and actions often center on the product. Kids of this generation hear these messages. As a parent, keep in mind that the process of working toward a goal is important because it teaches children the skills needed to become confident, independent, and thoughtful adults. It is important that children learn that overcoming the mistakes they make along the way to their goal is just as important as achieving the goal.

Putting It All Together

The Issue

Parents feel pressure to do everything right. Part of doing everything right is providing their children with every opportunity available to them. They feel they would be making a mistake if they didn't.

The Trap

Parents feel the pressure from early on to do everything right. Therefore, they often fall into the trap of fixing their children's mistakes, protecting them from taking chances that could lead to mistakes, and overscheduling them so they don't have time for mistakes.

The Alternative

The goal is to raise children who are confident, independent, and thoughtful, especially when it comes to solving problems independently. Remember to celebrate the mistakes and rejoice in knowing that, through practice, they will be much better equipped to take on their future.

1. Look at each problem as a positive opportunity for practice. Remember, the more practice they get solving the problem, the better they will be at it.
2. Talk about individual strengths and weaknesses as part of a whole person. No one is without challenges, and it is very valuable to praise how each challenge is overcome.
3. Don't overschedule your children. Give them the

responsibility to manage their free time. They need practice organizing unstructured time and priorities.

4. Make sure to praise the process toward meeting a goal as equally important to the goal being met. The following are some examples:

    a. "I am so proud of how dedicated you were to doing all the work so you could be recommended for the honors class."

    b. "You go to practice every day and love the competition of this sport. That is true commitment."

    c. "I know how hard that class was for you, and you really put in a lot of time toward studying."

    d. "I am really impressed with how responsible you were talking to your teacher about how you could pull your grade up."

Chapter 4
Understanding Developmental Stages

I was interviewing a parent who brought her son in for an ADHD evaluation. She was concerned about her son's lack of commitment to his responsibilities, such as school and cleaning his room. She wrote on one of the questionnaires that I use, "I am concerned about my constant reminders to him to stay on task. He asks for help when he doesn't need it. He isn't working his hardest to be the best he can be. If it gets done, it's because someone made him do it." She ended with, "I don't know how to help him become an independent learner." These seem like reasonable concerns for a parent to have, but in this case, the woman's son had recently turned six years old and just started first grade.

—Dr. Ron

As psychologists, we are excited to work with parents who want great things for their children and are willing to help them achieve their goals. But sometimes we have to remind parents about what is developmentally typical for their child's age, such as when parents ask for their children to be more insightful, perceptive, and mature than most children are at that age. The first grader mentioned earlier is capable of a lot of things, but he probably shouldn't be expected to be "working his hardest to be the best he can be," self-motivated, and an independent worker at the tender age of six. We wish we could say that scenario is unusual, but it isn't. With all the outside pressure for parents to make sure their kids have all the advantages possible, they often don't know what typical behavior is.

Most parents aren't confident in their barometer for knowing whether they are expecting enough or too much from their kids. When they are unsure, parents feel it is safer to push their kids ahead rather than risk them falling behind. That is one of the reasons it is so easy to fall into the trap of pushing kids too fast. It is possible to provide too much and push too hard, which results in kids missing out on valuable life lessons. In the first three chapters, we discussed the traps that cause parents to rescue their children. This chapter covers some simple guidelines that will help parents understand what can be expected of children at each developmental level, which will help parents to manage their own expectations. To do that, we venture into the basics of developmental stage theory.

Developmental Stage Theory

Developmental stage theory describes child development as a progression through distinct stages. Each stage is characterized by specific skills that are acquired during that stage and not before. Psychologists have been investigating this idea for decades, and some of the most famous and influential theorists have proposed their own ideas. Superstars such as John Bowlby, Sigmund Freud, Abraham Maslow, Erik Erikson, Margaret

Mahler, and Jean Piaget all spent significant time developing their own unique theories of development. Despite their individual perspectives, one area of agreement is that development occurs in a predictable sequence.

As psychologists, we find developmental stage theory guides our work with children and their families in many ways. Understanding what can be expected of children based on their age and developmental readiness is critical. We take into account each child's status in the realms of social, emotional, cognitive, educational, and physical development, and then we recommend interventions that are appropriate to his or her level. Sometimes the interventions are based on "typical" child development, and sometimes the interventions are geared toward a specific skill or set of skills that may be developing slower than expected. In both cases, the child's readiness is the driving factor.

Most of the prominent developmental stage theories encompass the entire life span, not just childhood. In this chapter, we have chosen three of the most well-known and researched theories to relate to child and adolescent development in this generation.

Theory No. 1: Social Development in Children

Erik Erikson's theory of psychosocial development is one of the most widely accepted in child psychology. It is centered on children and teens experiencing social challenges at different stages of their development.[1] If they are able to experience those challenges and figure out what to do, the outcome is growth and maturity.[2] The key here, as it is with all the theories, is that the child must *experience* the challenge. Take, for example, staying with a babysitter for the first time or deciding whom to eat lunch with on the first day of school. Both experiences are anxiety provoking and can result in either needing more practice or feeling good about the experience. Children are not required to master a challenge once; rather they develop their ability to master it over years. Kids try something, mess up, and figure out a new way to try the next time. Children's confidence in who they are and how they approach things in life is based on their ability to experience and figure out the challenges at each stage. If children have positive experiences and learn from the challenge, they progress to the next stage feeling confident in their skills. If children fail to master the challenge, they move on at a disadvantage, either with less confidence or with a misguided understanding of their role in social interactions. Children may continue to age physically, but socially and emotionally, they may be at a different stage than their peers.

The following are brief summaries of Erikson's psychosocial stages. You will see how development progresses naturally for most children.

1. **Infancy:** Erikson's first stage is infancy, which typically lasts from birth to eighteen months. The basic conflict encountered during this stage is called *trust vs. mistrust*. This fundamental stage revolves around basic needs; the infant is completely dependent on his caregiver for food, reliable care, and affection. The infant successfully builds trust if his caregiver is dependable, whereas inconsistent or emotionally unavailable caregivers will foster mistrust in the infant. If a child progresses through this stage with positive experiences, he will be more likely to trust others as he gets older.

2. **Early Childhood:** The second stage is early childhood, which typically lasts from eighteen months to three years of age. The basic conflict at this stage is *autonomy*

vs. shame and doubt. Children strive toward the development of a sense of independence and personal control over their environment and their own body. For example, a typical developmental step at this stage would be toilet training, which exemplifies control of one's own body and a sense of independence. You can see this fight for independence play out every day—such as when the child decides she suddenly doesn't like a certain food or doesn't want to nap. Another example might be the child who wants to walk up the stairs rather than be carried or get himself into his own car seat. If children do not begin to do things for themselves or they are prevented from doing so, they can develop a sense of shame and doubt about their ability to be independent and self-reliant. We all know there are times when it is just not possible to let toddlers do everything on their own. Doing something for your child is typical and will not impact this stage. Only when parents choose most of the time to do things for their children, rather than allow the toddler to develop a sense of autonomy, does this pose a problem.

3. **Preschool:** Erikson's third stage typically lasts from about three years old to five or six years old. The basic conflict at this age is called *initiative vs. guilt*. Independence and one's desire for exploration develop in this stage. Children begin to exert power over their environment by manipulating things around them. We see this opportunity for development during their play. Does a child initiate play or wait for other children to decide what they are going to do? Does the child share toys or take them and leave the area so others can't have them? They become more assertive and begin to initiate events rather than passively

wait for things to happen to them. When taking the initiative is successful, the child feels a sense of mastery and confidence, but the child who exerts too much or too little power may meet disapproval leading to feelings of guilt. Most often children don't know why their attempt at taking control was not accepted by others, but they feel bad or guilty that it wasn't successful. With practice, the child learns how to take initiative successfully.

As we discussed in chapter 3, the challenge with this generation of children is that parents are overinvolved in all aspects of their play. Parents are there to guide their children, tell them how to solve problems, and even speak for them if necessary. This overinvolvement or "hovering" inhibits the child's ability to figure out challenges on his own and learn from them. If children aren't given this chance, they are not going to progress through this stage with the confidence to take the initiative to try new things.

4. **School Age:** Erikson's fourth stage is thought to prevail from the ages of six to twelve years old. During this stage of development, the basic conflict is called *industry vs. inferiority,* and the important challenges and opportunities for development at this stage center on school. Not only are children faced with new academic demands, but the experience with more kids in structured and unstructured situations also increases the social demands placed on them. It is during these early school years that children learn how to make and keep friends in class (structured) and on the playground (unstructured). Success here leads a child to gain a sense of purpose and pride, while failure can result in feelings of inferiority. Children with a lot of friends seem more comfortable in new social situations,

probably because they know they have been able to make lots of friends in the past, while children without this skill show more anxiety. It is normal for children to experience some social conflicts, just as adults do. That is how they learn the skills to manage social dynamics. Children establish these skills slowly as they progress through the stage, making mistakes along the way. If they are not allowed to make those mistakes, then they don't develop the skills. Social conflicts are one of the most difficult things for parents to watch their child go through, which is why it is so tempting to jump in and rescue their kids.

5. **Adolescence:** According to Erikson, this stage lasts from twelve to eighteen years old, but current thinking on adolescence, based on actual brain development, extends it to the early twenties. The basic conflict for adolescents is *identity vs. role confusion* and is primarily related to peer relationships and a sense of self. They may experiment with physical appearance or behavior that they find interesting or intriguing. It is healthy for teens at this age to develop their own fashion sense, interest in music, and views about the world. They will then see how others respond to how they present themselves and decide how to react to that. Think about all the different "identities" you may have tried when you were going through this stage. Sometimes you were confident in your identity and other times you were confused. Since the goal is for a young person to develop her own identity, there is little chance it will be exactly what her parents were hoping for; but rest assured, it is healthy for her to create her own identity separate from parental expectations. Teens that develop a healthy sense of identity find it easier to remain

true to their belief in who they are while failure leads to role confusion and a weakened sense of self.

Most of us realize that how we identify ourselves and how we see the world changes throughout our adulthood as well. It is not necessary for a teen to enter his twenties knowing exactly who he is to be successful at this stage. What is important is having a sense of core values and beliefs that really help young people leave adolescence with confidence.

Consider Social Development When Parenting

A couple came to a session concerned that their son had told them many of his friends at school were swearing. The parents said that they told their child not to spend time with those friends at school and that they didn't think he should play together with those kids after school. I told them two things. First, it is typical for kids to experiment with swearing at that age. Second, it is so wonderful that their child is telling them this so they can help him navigate this new experience, not avoid it, or try to figure it out all alone. They can now help their son talk about why some kids swear, why adults don't want them to, and what he is going to do. If their child decides to swear too and does it around adults, he will experience the natural consequences that follow, but hopefully he will know the consequences as a result of having discussed this with them. This is a great learning experience. Trying to avoid any experience a parent thinks is "inappropriate" is futile and doesn't help a child learn.

—Dr. Darlene

Again, the most important and consistent factor in healthy psychosocial development is that children need to *experience* the challenge at each stage—even though watching children struggle socially can be difficult for parents. Parents must resist the temptation to rescue, push, overparent, and otherwise take over for their child.

Parents Can Support Social Development

According to Erikson, children need to move through a set of social challenges in order to become confident and develop their own identity.

- **Infancy:** The challenge for the infant is bonding with his caregivers. At this stage, parents should be loving, caring, and available. A secure bond between child and parents sets a great foundation for relationships with people the rest of his life.
- **Preschool:** The challenge for the child at this stage is the idea that it is OK to be away from her parents. Parents should encourage some separation and then express how proud they are of their child upon her return. A positive experience will build confidence.
- **School Age:** The challenge at this stage is making and keeping friends in less structured situations. Parents should feel comfortable letting their children practice playing away from them, such as at school playgrounds where it is safe and a caring adult is never too far away. If your child is experiencing social

challenges (such as kids not playing fairly or excluding your child), try not to solve his problems by going in and talking to school officials—unless safety is a concern. Instead, talk about the challenges at home with your child and find a way to have him practice with a close friend or sibling what he might do at school the next day.

- **Adolescence:** The goal in adolescence is for children to develop their own sense of who they are. Parents should expect some experimenting with hairstyles, dress, and views of the world. The parent who understands this process can support the child's attempt to be unique and independent without trying to control the child's form of expression. Parents should not panic when their teen expresses some minor rebellion but rather should focus their concerns on issues involving safety, such as drug use or reckless behavior.

Theory No. 2: Cognitive Development in Children

The mother of a five-year-old boy shared with me that she was concerned because he was very resistant anytime she asked him to say he was sorry for something he did. She was concerned he didn't care about the feelings of others. I was able to share with her that this was very common for kids his age. Most five-year-old children don't know how to consider the perspective of others. Therefore, when they are asked to say "sorry" they only know it is admitting they did something wrong, which makes them feel shameful

and anxious. They haven't developed the ability to under-
stand that saying sorry is more about helping the other
person feel better.

—Dr. Darlene

Another one of the most widely accepted and popular theories on cognitive development was proposed by Jean Piaget. Piaget's stage theory focuses on the way children's thinking becomes more advanced as they get older.[3] According to Piaget, children work through a series of four stages in which they experience a change in how they understand the world. He described children as little scientists exploring the world around them.

Like Erikson, Piaget believed that children construct their own knowledge about themselves and the world based on their experiences, but he looked at how a child's *thinking* changes as he or she progresses through development. Piaget proposed that kids learn primarily on their own, without the intervention of parents and adults. He also found that children were intrinsically motivated and didn't need rewards from adults to seek learning. Here are Piaget's four stages:

1. **Sensorimotor:** The first stage is from birth to two years old. In this stage, children learn from the sensations that result from their movements. A prominent development is that children in this stage learn that they exist separately from the people and the objects around them. For example, children learn that things continue to exist even when they can't see them. This means that when a parent leaves the room, the child understands that they still exist. Children also learn that they can cause things to happen in their environment. For example, if a six-month-old

baby wants a toy, she may scoot, crawl, or cry to get it. Each time she is successful in getting what she wants, it reinforces her confidence to try again.

2. **Preoperational:** The second stage lasts from approximately two years old until seven years old. It starts with children developing language as a positive way to communicate with others. You will notice people begin telling children at this age to "use your words." That is because that is exactly what they are ready to learn to do: not just increasing their vocabulary but expressing more advanced thoughts and feelings. They also learn to count and classify objects. Children in this stage are primarily concrete thinkers and are not yet able to utilize abstract concepts. Their thinking is egocentric, meaning they believe everyone sees the world from the same perspective as they do. However, they begin to utilize past and future thinking.

   This stage can be a tough one for parents, because their children are beginning to understand the consequences of their behavior, but they don't typically see things from the perspective of the parent or anyone else. Therefore, when assisting children with problems, parents are going to need to help them see that perspective. We'll provide tips on how to do this at the end of this section.

3. **Concrete Operations:** Piaget's third stage lasts from seven years old until about eleven years old. Children in this stage begin to be able to see things from the perspective of other people and can focus on events that occur outside their own lives. They begin to think more logically and gain a better understanding of mental operations such as hypothetical questions. They are also less egocentric. Therefore, problem solving becomes a more rational

process, albeit still concrete. Children at this age thrive in environments that give them the chance to increase their independence and figure things out on their own.

4. **Formal Operations:** The final stage of Piaget's theory starts at about eleven or twelve years old and really focuses on an increase in logic, reasoning, and abstract thinking. Children at this age begin to apply math and science concepts to help make decisions about hypothetical situations. They also make use of advanced problem-solving skills such as planning and prioritizing, and the consideration of possible outcomes of their actions. This enables them to predict ahead of time, with some certainty, the results of their actions. This is a time when there is significant growth and development in the way children think about things, which is a good time for them to be exposed to opportunities to take chances, make mistakes, and learn how to fix those mistakes.

Consider Cognitive Development When Parenting

I met with a mother and father who asked me to do a reading evaluation on their six-year-old daughter. The parents explained: "She is in a lower reading group than her friends at school and it seems like she is far behind the other kids." The results of the evaluation showed that the girl had an average reading ability and no reading problems. I shared with the parents that there were probably some exceptional readers in her class and that she was developing these early reading skills at her own pace. I asked her parents to let me know by the end of the year if things had improved or stayed the same. The feedback

several months later was, "I think something just clicked with her and now she is doing great at reading."
                                                                    —Dr. Ron

According to Piaget, children develop cognitive skills in phases that last several years at a time, which means there is a wide range of what is considered the "typical" time for a child to develop any one skill. In addition, children develop these skills gradually, not all at once. This means it can sometimes look like their development is uneven, which can be confusing for parents. When children make good choices in one situation, but not another, it can look like they are being careless, when in reality the new skills have simply not been developed enough to be used consistently.

As we saw in chapter 1, in this generation, well-intentioned parents get caught up in the pressure to push their children too hard too soon. A concrete example of this is a parents' focus on their child being an early reader. Early enrichment and exposure to reading and the alphabet is great, but you simply can't rush a child's readiness for reading. Teachers tell us all the time that parents get anxious and upset with their children when they are on the slower side to acquire this skill. They remind parents that some kids are simply ready to read earlier than others and that this difference diminishes by second grade. In fact, they share that the kids who are supported in reading at their developmental level actually build a stronger comprehension of what they read because they are not pushed too far ahead of where they should be. Chapter 2 taught us that anxious parents also tend to jump in and rescue their children from taking on the responsibilities they are fully capable of handling. Today's parents mean well, but ultimately are not doing their children any favors by sheltering and protecting them from natural, developmentally typical struggles. The core of cognitive development is learning through experience and practice. Throughout childhood, we face countless developmental milestones. Most kids meet these challenges with some struggle, but naturally come to master the skill needed to progress. Knowing a little bit about cognitive development should help parents understand that their children's struggles with new concepts are very natural. It is important to support a child's learning, not replace his or her learning. Be patient!

Parents Can Support Cognitive Development

- **Sensorimotor Development:** Parents of infants and toddlers should support their child's efforts to explore his or her environment. Understand that at this age children explore through touching, tasting, and smelling everything they can get their hands on. Parents should be aware of potential safety issues such as a child getting into cleaning supplies, touching electric outlets, and exploring in places where he can get hurt, but other than that they should enjoy watching their children learn about the world around them.

- **Preoperational Development:** The goal for children of preschool to early elementary age is the improvement of their language skills and their attempt to organize their world in a concrete way. Parents should gear their expectations to a level appropriate to their child, such as keeping in mind the limitations on advanced problem solving at this age. Parents will need to help their children learn to express their thoughts and feelings about things using the newly emerging skills of their children. This may require some coaching on the part of the parent. They should not do the talking for their child, but direct coaching at this age is very appropriate.

- **Concrete Operations:** Children are occupied with the concrete operations stage of development from older elementary school through middle school. By this point, kids are beginning to develop advanced problem-solving skills. They should be encouraged to take on additional responsibilities. This is a great age to let them try to do things their way and experience the outcome, since the consequences are likely going to be minor. That makes these wonderful "practice years." They are capable of critical thinking and should be encouraged to use that skill. Ask them questions that require them to "think" and have fun talking about whatever their response is. The questions can be about anything: how a rock got on top of a mountain or what kind of music they and their friends like. It is important to remember not to be critical of their thinking because that may discourage them from wanting to share their thoughts with you anymore.

- **Formal Operations:** Adolescents can absorb lots of information and make use of the most important data to make decisions. They can also see that their behavior and actions impact others. Consequently, parents can reasonably expect their adolescent children to use those abilities. They are able to consider issues on a global level, and parents can really enjoy hearing their outlook on societal events. Make sure to listen with an open and nonjudgmental mind. The key to keeping your teen talking is to be a good listener. Thus listening to your children can help them develop cognitively through the formal operations phase of life.

Theory No. 3: Moral Development in Children

Lawrence Kohlberg's most significant contribution to developmental stage theory is in the area of moral development.[4] In contrast to Erikson and Piaget, Kohlberg put almost no emphasis on an individual's age and focused on their needs and motives. His famous research focused on the responses that individuals gave on a series of moral dilemmas.[5] Essentially, he would ask people what they would do in a particularly difficult situation in which there was no clear answer. For instance, knowing that it was against the law and immoral, he asked people if they would steal food to feed their family, if they had no money to pay for it. Based on the responses collected through hundreds of interviews with people of all ages, Kohlberg was able to classify moral reasoning in a sequence of six stages grouped into three general levels of morality. He was most interested in how people solved the dilemma, not what the response was. As you read about the stages, notice how they coincide with Erikson and Piaget's stages. You will see that a child needs to be emotionally and cognitively ready to process the moral dilemmas of each stage.

Level I: Preconventional Morality
Stage 1
This stage is thought of as *obedience and punishment* and is evidenced in preschool and most early elementary school children. At this stage, kids make decisions based on what suits their needs, and they don't yet consider the needs or feelings of others. Instead, rules are followed because authority figures (parents and teachers) make and enforce them. From a child's view, a behavior is morally wrong if he or she will be punished for it.

Stage 2
This stage is *self-interest* driven. At this point, children begin to recognize that other people have needs, just as they do. Further, children learn that one way to get what they want is to give other people what they want in return. Kids are still driven by consequences to determine right from wrong, but they consider how to get others to get them what they want. The analogy "I'll scratch your back if you scratch mine" is often used to describe actions at this stage.

Level II: Conventional Morality
Stage 3
This stage is more *conformity* driven and is typical of many adolescents, including middle school and high school students. At this level, individuals examine society's views and expectations and validate the morality of their actions based on the actions of others. There is an acceptance of the rules and norms of society even when there is no overt consequence for the action or behavior. Adolescents focus on maintaining relationships, earning trust, and developing loyalty within their relationships.

Stage 4

This stage is about knowing *right from wrong*. At this point, people transition to a level of moral decision making that is beyond the need for approval from others and is based more on the totality of the action. This tends to happen in high school and young adulthood, and for many people this is the most complex level of moral development they will reach. People understand the need for laws and rules because of their role in maintaining order in society. Even if they disagree with the law, they understand that it is morally wrong to break it. They see rules as inflexible, and often fail to recognize that as society changes, so should the rules.

Level III: Postconventional Morality

Stage 5

This stage is considered the *social contract*, where it is understood that everyone has his or her own opinions and values. This level of reasoning is typically not seen before reaching college age. Laws are viewed as useful social contracts, but are not rigid. They represent civil order, but not absolute moral stances, and should be changed as needed based on a changing society. Stages 4 and 5 are the highest levels of moral development that most people reach.

Stage 6

This stage is the *ideal or universal* morality, and few people ever reach this level. It is often thought of as a "hypothetical" stage in that it involves a strong inner conscience and willingness to violate one's own ethical principles for a greater good. At this level, there would be no need for rules or laws as everyone would do what was right at all times, but that requires everyone to be at this level. Because many people don't reach this level of morality, it would be unsafe to depend on this kind of advanced moral reasoning in today's society.

Consider Moral Development When Parenting

Parent: Dr. Stolberg, I need some help. My eight-year-old son follows all our rules at home and is generally helpful and considerate. But when he visits his best friend's house, he does things that make me want to pull my hair out. I am sure he knows better because he never does these things with that same boy at our house. Why does he behave this way away from our home?

Dr. Ron: He probably wasn't mature enough to do what was "right" simply because it was the "right" thing to do. Instead, he was likely responding differently based on the rules of each house. In the house with clear rules and consequences, he meets the expectations to avoid the punishment, but at his friend's house, things are probably not so clear to him, so he does whatever his friend does. In fact, it is probably pretty confusing to him that he can do something that is OK at his friend's house, but be punished for it at his own house.

The development of moral reasoning is not based on what age or grade a child is in. It is a representation of how they see the world and get their needs met. As parents, we all look for that point when our children learn to do what is right because it is right, not because they will get in trouble if they don't do the right thing.

Without knowing it, parents use the development of moral

reasoning to make a lot of decisions regarding their children. There comes a time when we trust them to walk or ride a bike to school, to do their homework without us checking it, and to stay out late into the evenings with their friends on a weekend. Most likely, the child or teen has demonstrated to a parent that she can be trusted in these situations to follow the rules or to make well-thought-out decisions. Obviously, the better they prove to us that they are responsible and trustworthy, the more privileges we give them.

With the other developmental theories discussed here, we have demonstrated how even the most considerate parents may try to rush their children through a developmental challenge because they see other kids mastering it, or provide so much support that a child doesn't really get exposed to the challenge. The same concept applies to moral development. Children simply need to move through the stages as they grow and gain lots of practice. Parents cannot do this for their kids, they can't rush it, and they shouldn't protect them from the process.

Essentially, kids need to make mistakes. With young children, it might be a little thing like not sharing a toy and making a playmate cry, and with teens, it could involve theft, cheating in school, or lying. Parents in these situations are tempted to jump in and resolve the problem for their children. Regardless of what the moral dilemma is, children need the opportunity to learn from their mistakes and evaluate their behavior and value set.

I was working with a high school boy who cheated on a test at school. The teacher sent a note home to the parents asking them to sign the test acknowledging that they were informed of the violation and return it to school. The teen never showed his parents the test and signed their name without permission. When the teacher called home because she was suspicious about the signature, the father didn't want his son to get suspended for cheating so he admitted to signing the test.

—Dr. Ron

This high schooler could have been presented with an opportunity to develop a greater level of moral development. Instead, his parents were too concerned with the implications of cheating in school to let their son experience not only the punishment for cheating but the deeper moral lesson. If he were allowed to experience shame and the resulting embarrassment of disappointing the adults in his life, then he would have had the chance to grow from that experience. He would then have been able to work to earn back their trust, which is empowering and leads to stronger moral character. Instead, he was denied that chance and left with being rewarded for what he did.

Parents Can Support Moral Development

Moral development is less dependent on the age of the individual and focuses on the thinking and problem-solving skills they have developed.

- **Preconventional Morality:** At this phase, children respond to situations based on the rules and consequences surrounding them, which determines right and wrong. Parents can help by developing clear and concise rules and consistently applying accompanying consequences. Children respond best when they know what their parents' response is going to be.

- **Conventional Morality:** Children at this phase are focused on conformity to a peer group. At this age, kids adopt the group's sense of responsibility, views about the world, and how they will treat each other, which means a child's peer group will have a powerful influence on the thinking and moral development of a child. Parents who are around to observe during activities that include their child's friends are at a big advantage. Opportunities for observing include driving children and their friends to events and hosting the group at their house. Being able to discuss the difference between the family's values and those of their peers with your child is a valuable tool to open communication.

- **Postconventional Morality:** This phase of moral development and thinking seldom occurs before college, but parents of children of any age can be supportive of this process. It is at this point that individuals begin to see morality as being a responsibility to society and not just about laws and rules. Supporting a child's drive to change how they interact with society and the rules of a community is very important.

Parenting with a Purpose

You will notice that at the core of all these theories is the need for children, teens, and young adults to experience challenges in order to develop the skills to move on to the next stage successfully. The process relies on children's thinking to change as their brains develop and they are subjected to a wide range of experiences. Whether parents are pushing their children too fast through the stages or protecting them so much that their children don't get to experience them, kids in this generation are missing the opportunity to practice the skills that are learned as they progress through each stage of development.

Putting It All Together

The Issue
Everyone wants to be the best parent he or she can be. In doing so, parents want their children to meet the high expectations they set for their children to be bright, socially gifted, and of high moral character.

The Trap
When parents aren't aware of the typical course of social, cognitive, and moral development of children, their expectations can exceed their child's ability and readiness—with adverse consequences for the child.

The Alternative
Be aware of where your children fall in each developmental level and have reasonable expectations for them at every age. As children are moving through each stage, parents can foster learning experiences and challenges that are stage appropriate.

It is important to remember that children can be at different levels of social, cognitive, or moral development at the same time. Compared to their peers, they may be very advanced in one or two areas and lagging a bit behind in others. Feel free to support them, but try not to rescue them, because they need the struggle to achieve each new level or milestone in development.

CHAPTER 5

Take Advantage of the Critical Periods of Brain Development

We frequently hear about conflicts that deal with a child's inability to print out a school assignment. This is such a common source of anxiety for students and parents alike. For example, the student goes to print out the assignment and the household printer is out of ink or won't work, and he or she immediately begins to panic. The student can just as easily print in another color, save it on a jump drive to print at school, stop at a copy center on the way to school, print at the library or at a friend's house; there are lots of options. But the immediate reaction is hopelessness, rather than creative problem solving.

—Dr. Darlene and Dr. Ron

In past generations, there were natural opportunities every day for children and teens to practice the skills discussed in this book. In fact, there was no way around it. Think about the difference in freedom that children in the 1960s, '70s, and '80s had in planning their days. Many of you may remember the phrase, "Be home when the street lights come on." Parents often didn't know where their children were from the time they left the house to the time it was dark. While they were gone, they were organizing games, playing with other children, and, yes, getting into mischief. All those things required practice with essential skills that would be used throughout their lives: organization, planning, and using judgment to make decisions. These opportunities enhanced brain development, flexible thinking, and independent problem solving. On the other hand, many children in this generation are deprived of those same experiences. Whether it is concern about safety, lack of free time in a schedule, or too much homework, kids do not have the same freedoms and, therefore, the same opportunities as in previous generations.

Not only are today's children overscheduled and given fewer opportunities for independence, but the advancements in technology have also taken away even more opportunities for children to practice essential life skills. When the solution for a problem comes in seconds because a child picks up a phone to call someone or Google it, they are not required to think for themselves and figure things out. Children and teens are becoming reliant on technology to give them answers and have difficulty coming up with solutions without it.

In addition to the scenarios of children being out on their own, there are many other opportunities to practice thinking and problem solving that are also lost to this generation because of the convenience of technology. Let's compare how everyday experiences for children and teens differ now from the year 1999.

	Then	Now
Video technology	To record a favorite TV show you needed to know when it was on, which channel, set the VCR, and remember not to accidentally record over the cassette tape. If there were two shows on at the same time, family members needed to carefully negotiate which show they would record. This gave children an opportunity to develop interpersonal skills, such as communication and compromise, as well as independent planning and organization.	Almost every show is available immediately any time of day or night on demand, no thought required.
Map skills	In the glove compartment of most cars, you could find a state map or U.S. atlas. If you got lost when driving, you would need to look at a map, figure out if the neighborhood was safe to ask directions, and try to follow the directions. This gave teens the opportunity to learn how to deal with an unexpected outcome by using problem-solving, decision-making, social-reasoning, and communication skills.	GPS will lead the way, or if per chance you do get lost, a quick call on a cell phone (or a driving directions app like Google Maps) would identify your location and route in seconds. No problem solving is needed—just savvy smartphone skills.

	Then	Now
Research skills	To complete a research paper, you would need to plan a trip to the library; find what book, encyclopedia, or journal would contain the information you wanted; take notes on the information or photocopy the source; and check out books to bring home from the library (and remember to return them when finished). This allowed children to learn how to manage their time, figure out how to gather and organize the materials, and take responsibility to return the materials to the library on time.	Type any term or phrase into an Internet search engine on a computer in the convenience of your home, and all the information is at your fingertips in an instant. No planning is needed.

This list can go on and on. We are thankful for the ways technology makes getting lost safer and offers unlimited information when we want to learn about something new. But if you look at the countless ways this generation is missing opportunities to develop cognitive skills (problem solving, planning, organization, and communication) that people in past generations had every day, you can see that children and teens are entering the adult world substantially unprepared. This chapter focuses on the cognitive development that is negatively impacted by the lack of practice of invaluable skills.

As things become easier and easier for the Instant Gratification Generation, the primary neurological development that is essential in preparing children for self-reliance and decision making is deprived. This can be observed in their reactions to problems: they feel hopeless, rather than take the initiative to solve problems.

Theories on Cognitive Development

There is a reason educators and child psychologists learn and continue to use developmental theories that were derived in the 1920s and 1950s.[1] As discussed in chapter 4, theorists have identified stages of development that are consistent across generations and cultures. This is also true for theories that address brain development and how children solve problems.

As is typically the case, new research and theories continue to develop. However, the premise for each of these theories remains the same. They all agree that brain development is a relatively stable process—it occurs in a predictable order that is consistent across the majority of children. More specifically, they agree that development cannot be rushed and children are limited in how they think about things depending on their age, maturity, and developmental stage.

Let's use the example of sharing. This is an important lesson that parents teach to their young children. When older children and adults think about sharing, they consider it in relation to how it makes the other person feel. They may think about whether it makes the other person feel happy and accepted if something is shared or left out and angry if it is not. On the other hand, when preschool children begin to share, they do it because they learn that they are praised for sharing or because they are told to share. They don't inherently want to share; they just know other people smile and say, "Good job!" when they do, and they like the positive attention. Parents can try to force them to understand the true meaning of sharing, but young children are not neurologically, socially, or morally ready to learn it yet. Rest assured, there comes a time when all these messages have meaning, but it will be in the appropriate developmental stage.

Reinforce Your Child's Skills with Praise

Young children may not understand why their parents are asking them to behave in a certain way, but they learn very quickly that they are praised when they do. For example, a young child will not understand that sharing, saying "please" and "thank you," and taking turns makes the other person feel good. But they will quickly learn that they receive a lot of positive praise when they do. So they do those things for the praise. That is great! It encourages them to continue to do those things, which continues to lead to a positive outcome. When they are developmentally ready to understand the interpersonal meaning of those actions, they will experience it with pride and confidence.

Brain Development

The increase of convenience and instant gratification in this generation not only impacts the ability of children and teens to develop skills through practice but also affects brain development. Without exposure to experiences for them to practice considering other people's feelings, thinking about the consequences of behavior before acting, and independently solving problems, their brains are not strengthening the connections needed for learning and using these skills. Let's demonstrate this through learning how the brain develops and grows.

While there are some parts of brain development that are stable and only develop with physical maturation, there are other parts of brain function that can be advanced with practice. This is not unlike learning to play a musical instrument, or learning to speak a language, body building, or developing any other skill that we can master through regular practice. There is a critical time in a child's life when skills and abilities are more easily developed if he is exposed to experiences that promote that type of learning. The *critical period* is a "specific stage in human development during which certain types of behavior normally are shaped and molded."[2] In other words, it is the time in maturation when experiences have their peak effect on learning.

During the critical period, synapses are developing at an accelerated rate—more quickly than any other time in a person's life—which is called *synaptic overproduction*. This is the peak learning time when the brain is ready to take in all manner of stimuli. During the period of synaptic overproduction, the connections between synapses are enhanced by experience. The more a skill is practiced, the more the brain develops in that area.

On the one hand, while practice and experience strengthen connections, on the other hand synapses that are not used are "pruned" away. This means that if children are not exposed to the experience that is critical to that time in learning, those synapses wither. Put simply, synapses follow the "use it or lose it" philosophy. While it is possible to learn the skill later, it is much more difficult.

The best way to show this is through the well-documented critical period for language acquisition.[3] Infants and toddlers rapidly develop connections to process sounds because that is what is happening in that critical period.[4] They go from nonverbal to fluently verbal in just a couple of years. The more infants and toddlers are exposed to language, the stronger the synapses that process the sounds of language become. The connections for sounds a child doesn't hear are decreased (pruned). Along the same lines, a child who is exposed to more than one language early on will develop stronger connections to more sounds and maintain those connections than a child who is only exposed to a single language.

People can still learn additional languages outside the critical period; it is just a more arduous process. Think about how easy it is for a bilingual person to learn a third language. Building a foundation for multiple languages allows a person to learn similar skills more naturally later on. The same also holds true for other neurological processes, such as problem solving.

Parents of this generation tend to get very caught up in trying to push their children ahead and protect them from making mistakes or being unhappy. In doing so, parents prevent their children from being exposed to the experiences that are critical to the developmental stage they are in at that time. If children aren't exposed during the optimal times, it is much more difficult to master the skills when they are older. Parents who push their kids too fast or insulate them do just that. On the other hand, parents who allow their children to fix their own mistakes, be active in decision making, take on responsibilities, and work for things they have are actively exposing them to the needed experiences for stronger executive functioning.

Executive Functioning

Executive functioning may be one of the most important things for children and teens to practice in preparation for adulthood. Executive functioning is the ability to use higher order reasoning to manage and utilize multiple pieces of information to solve problems and make decisions. This includes the ability to plan, organize, multitask, and distinguish important from unimportant information.

When we interviewed parents about what skills they really want to teach their children before they launch into adulthood, they listed things such as good social skills, independent thinking, being considerate, and having a strong work ethic as the primary characteristics. These skills are all related to executive functioning. Think about what adults are required to do every day. In any given day, you may need to manage not only your schedule but the schedule of your family members; complete all the daily living skills for yourself (e.g., shower, dress, eat); find time for errands; take care of children; work (which includes a whole list of additional executive-functioning requirements); remember to return phone calls and reply to email and text messages; and manage appointments (yours, hers, his, theirs). Executive functioning is at the core of independent, considerate, and self-sufficient functioning.

At a more complex level, executive functioning allows a person to be flexible and adaptive in his thinking. It is great to have a plan, but often things don't go according to plan. Executive functioning is what enables a person to adapt to unexpected outcomes, change plans, and make new ones, all while considering the other people who may be involved. When considering that the ultimate goal for parents is to raise children who are prepared for college and adult life, you can see how important these skills are.

Let's take the typical week of many college students. First, they are required to maintain their structured schedule of classes, mealtimes, appointments, and so on. This is often the easy part because they are used to following a schedule of activities. The bigger challenge is the requirement to also independently plan for their other responsibilities.

- Professors typically give a tentative schedule for the entire semester that needs to be integrated into daily activity. For example, a professor may say that on a specific date two months away, there will be a midterm on the first ten chapters of a textbook. That means reading one to two chapters per week and then leaving time to learn what was read. And that is just one class.
- Students also need to plan time to complete assignments, read, write papers, and study for all four or five classes in which they are enrolled.
- If there are difficulties in a class, the professor most likely will not approach them. It is left to the students to ask for help.
- Students need to fit in personal responsibilities, such as laundry, personal hygiene, and grocery shopping.
- They need to independently manage their money. For many students this is the first time they will do this on their own, and for most students it is the first time they need to account for all their personal expenses as well as extracurricular expenses.
- Social pressures are prominent for many college students, including sharing a room (often for the first time), meeting many new people, and learning how to balance the freedom of social life with other responsibilities.

It is not just one skill the student is required to use; it is all of them at the same time. They won't have anyone asking if they finished their homework or telling them to come home early because they have class the next morning. They also won't have anyone there to help them recover from a meltdown when they are overwhelmed. In high school, parents often emphasize the importance of their child's SAT scores and GPA, which of course play a role in getting accepted to a good college. But once they are college students, it will not be their SAT scores or GPA that will help them. It will be executive functioning.

Parents who allow their children to figure out a problem before jumping in to rescue them are helping them develop executive functioning. So are parents who are encouraging extra responsibility in childhood by expecting their children to work for things they want. In chapter 6, you'll find a list of characteristics that teachers believe are the most important predictors of college success. The most common characteristics include resilience, critical thinking, and a willingness to take responsibility. Notice that these are all related to executive functioning.

Optimal Learning for Executive Functioning

A couple came in with their seventeen-year-old daughter and wanted to discuss laundry responsibilities in the house. The girl was getting frustrated with her mother because her mom did not wash and hang her clothes the way she liked. The couple then told her that she could do her own laundry, which was just fine with the girl because she was trying to establish as much independence from her parents as she could (very developmentally typical as she was preparing to leave for college the next year). The problem came when, despite the agreement, Mom washed her school uniform every time the girl forgot. She was angry that her mom was going into her stuff and Mom was frustrated she was not thankful that she helped her. Mom told me, "What if she goes to school with dirty clothes or gets in trouble for not wearing her uniform?" My answer was, "Wouldn't you rather this happen now while she can learn from the natural consequences and develop better planning skills, rather than when she is in college dealing with a whole bunch of other new skills to learn?" This is a perfect example of a missed opportunity to learn from experience and develop the executive-functioning skills during the critical time of adolescence.

—Dr. Darlene

Research has shown that the optimal learning period for executive functioning occurs between middle school and into the early twenties. The frontal lobe region is the primary area of the brain that controls executive functioning. This region interfaces and interacts with multiple other areas of the brain. While many areas of the brain develop throughout childhood, the frontal lobe develops rapidly in early adolescence and continues into young adulthood. Early adolescents and young adults, therefore, are capable of being more independent in managing their work at school, caring for their personal items, and balancing other responsibilities such as chores or a part-time job.

In their article, "Development of the Adolescent Brain: Implications for Executive Function and Social Cognition," Sarah-Jayne Blakemore and Suparna Choudhury provide a very nice summary of the neurological development of children and adolescents, including the changes that occur throughout childhood.[5] They provide a comprehensive review of research that clearly documents the consistency of findings by using neuro-imaging and neurological tests. They also include research that looks at brain development over time.

One of the most fascinating and timely findings is the synaptic reorganization in the areas of executive functioning and social cognition that occurs during puberty. Blakemore and Choudhury showed clearly through the summary of research that during puberty, adolescents not only are the most ready to learn executive-functioning skills but also are the most ready to apply these skills to their social relationships. Puberty is the critical time to learn these skills, and they learn best through personal experience. Therefore, when parents fall into the trap of rescuing them from solving problems on their own, jumping in to smooth the way in social situations, or giving them things without them working for it, valuable experiential opportunities are taken away. Adolescence is when their brains are primed to integrate and learn from all they are experiencing as well as when these skills will be learned more easily than at any other time. This is why these skills need to be a top priority when parenting and educating children and teens.

What some parents don't realize is that while they are seeking academic advancement and extra tutoring to push their kids ahead in preparation for college and adulthood, they are bypassing the essential skills to be learned during adolescence. If adolescents are not given ample opportunity to independently experience and practice planning, organization, making decisions, and critical thinking during this time, they will be entering adulthood vastly unprepared.

Confidence Comes with Experience

While the brain is primed to learn executive functioning beginning in middle school, by no means should
parents wait until then to help them prepare for these
experiences. Even at young ages, children should learn
to expect the response, "What do you think you should
do?" from their parents when they approach their parents with a problem.

- A toddler shows her dad a broken toy and his
  answer can be, "How do you think we can fix it?"
- An eight-year-old forgot a math sheet for homework
  and the prompt is, "What is the best way to solve
  this problem?"
- A ten-year-old talks about a conflict with another
  child at school and the guidance is, "What are some
  things you can do to make that interaction better?"

The solutions are usually not going to be well
developed or mature and will likely need some support
from an adult, but this response helps them become
comfortable with the idea that they are the ones who
need to come up with solutions when there is a problem, not someone else. This enables them to build the
confidence they will need to tackle the challenge of
developing the more complex skills of executive functioning later on.

How Parents Can Promote Good Judgment and Decision Making

The use of good judgment when making decisions requires a person to exhibit positive executive functioning, as well as the ability to be considerate and aware of others. Just as with anything else, there are some children who are naturally gifted at this, beginning at a young age. However, most children need lots and lots of practice with decision-making skills—it's a process that develops slowly over time.

For example, when an elementary school–aged child puts on a seatbelt every time she gets in the car or wears a helmet every time she rides a bike, it seems like she is making good decisions based on sound judgment. In reality, the child is following a well-established habit. Young kids fail to fully understand the importance of wearing a seatbelt or helmet in an accident, even though their parents explain that it is good for them. There is a difference between doing something out of habit and using good judgment.

Young children first learn behaviors based on habit and repetition, what authority figures have told them to do, and what they have observed. Sometime in late elementary school, they also begin to learn from personal experience and practice. When a routine or habit changes, they are required to rely on the executive-functioning skills of identifying alternative solutions, considering how the solutions will impact others, which of the solutions will have the best outcome, and then figuring out how to implement the solution. Today's Instant Gratification Generation habitually jumps at the first possible solution, rather than considering all the potential outcomes. That impulsive need for an immediate solution prevents them from using good judgment when making decisions. In turn, if a parent falls in the rescue trap, kids are prevented from problem solving on their own.

One way parents fall into the rescue trap is by telling them about mistakes they made as a kid, in hopes their own children won't make the same ones. Adults have a lot of experience making mistakes and learning from them, which helps us to avoid doing the same thing again. As psychologists, we hear all the time, "I don't want them to make the same mistakes I did." So how do teens learn?

- Some particularly mature and conscientious teens learn by listening to their parents and feeling sympathy for what their parents went through.
- Others learn by watching someone in their peer group experience something, including the outcomes and consequences (positive and negative).
- The most salient learning comes from direct personal experience. Many teens have an "it will never happen to me" mind-set and act accordingly. Those are the ones who need to experience the consequences of a situation and learn from that (i.e., oh, it can happen to me).

Parents of kids in this generation need to be even more aware of how they can encourage their children to take advantage of this critical period of learning. This promotes brain development in the child (building stronger synaptic connections) in the area of executive functioning.

How to Preview Consequences with Your Child or Teen

Giving your teenager space to experience things can be really scary for a parent. Previewing consequences as much as possible can be an effective communication tool, because this establishes your expectations as a parent, and clarifies potential outcomes for your teen. Here are some examples of what you can say:

- "If you miss curfew, you will not be able to go out with your friends for two weeks."
- "If there is drinking at the party, you can call us and we will pick you up. If you don't call and we find out about it, you will not be able to go out with your friends for two weeks."
- "If we find that you had friends in the car (before legally able, a huge problem in California), you will lose car privileges for a month."
- "If you make a decision that puts you or someone else in an unsafe situation, you will face very serious consequences."

The Most Important Lessons

In the Instant Gratification Generation, children and teens are missing the essential opportunity to practice the skills that parents, teachers, researchers, and employers deem the most important. Practice takes work and time, is not convenient, and can cause a lot of frustration. Yet it is essential to provide opportunities to teach children and teens that most things take practice to do well. This idea is the subject of the article by Rachel Keen, "The Development of Problem Solving in Young Children: A Critical Cognitive Skill." This important review of development concludes that parents and society as a whole need to design opportunities and environments that encourage and enhance problem solving for children as early as the first year of life.[6] That there is evidence that children as young as one and two are capable of early problem-solving strategies surprises many people.

If parents understand the importance of taking advantage of the critical period of adolescence to build a foundation and solidify problem-solving skills, their children will be much better prepared for college and the adult world. It is so important when raising and educating children and teens of this generation to realize the ways that overscheduling, dependence on technology, and rewarding the end product rather than hard work undermines the natural developmental process that teens in past generations had the chance to experience naturally. The best gift you can give your children is ample practice to learn how to think.

Putting It All Together

The Issue
This generation of children and teens is so technologically advanced that they have the ability to use electronics to solve many of their problems for them. In addition, parents tend to emphasize the academic résumé and providing their children advantages at the expense of taking advantage of the "critical period" for developing executive functioning, which are the skills that are so essential to becoming a confident, independent, and thoughtful adult.

The Trap
In this generation, it is so easy to get caught up in the traps that limit the development of executive functioning: rescuing

children, solving their problems for them, giving them things without them working for it, and becoming reliant on the ease and convenience of technology.

The Alternative

Be supportive of your child's efforts to solve problems and think critically, even if his solutions are not well developed. Remember that children do not always comprehend the complexities of their social and emotional environments. By providing them with opportunities to practice these skills, you are equipping them with tools that will last a lifetime.

1. Emphasize mistakes as part of the process of learning to solve problems.
2. Praise your children when they try to do things for themselves.
3. Focus on the "process" and effort your child puts toward a task, rather than the outcome, even if the outcome wasn't what she expected. That means talking about how she tried to achieve a goal and whether or not it worked. If not, what could she have done differently?
4. Avoid focusing on things such as "honors class" or "competitive athletic team" as accomplishments. Instead, focus on the work a child needs to put toward getting there.
5. Don't put your child's academic résumé ahead of learning to solve problems, don't manage his or her schedule, and encourage your child to take chances to try new things.

When working with teens, especially those who feel they know better than their parents, very often the best way to help them develop their skills is to let them learn from natural consequences.

1. Don't do the work for your teen; let her experience the disappointment, guilt, and consequences of failing to study for an exam or complete an assignment.

2. If you know your teen is going to need a particular outfit or item for school (or anything else), feel free to ask if he needs help getting it. If you get ignored, leave him to find a way to deal with his lack of planning or laziness. He will have to figure out something. If this results in embarrassment or stress, your teen probably won't let it happen again. Don't take the bait and do it for him without being asked.

3. Preview the consequences of choices they will be required to make, such as missing curfew, getting a poor grade, cutting class, drinking alcohol, being unkind, not being at the place they told you, and so on.

CHAPTER 6

Ivy League or Bust

Are We Providing Children What They Really Need to Succeed?

Parent: Dr. Stolberg, I am calling to see if you can help our son. He went to college this year and is having a hard time. He wants to come home. He always got good grades and took lots of AP classes in high school, but now he is failing his classes. He said he wants to take a year off and transfer to another school next year.

Most parents will agree that having their children earn an advanced degree after high school is high on their list of child-rearing goals. In fact, nationally, the emphasis on promoting higher education has become a top priority. The United States spends more on higher education than any other nation in the world, and that financial commitment increases each year. Yet 30 percent of students beginning a four-year college do not return after the first year and only 60 percent of students attending a four-year college complete their degree in four years.[1]

We receive many calls every year from parents whose college-aged children are struggling with their adult responsibilities.

Parents list the student's accomplishments and express surprise and frustration that their child is not following the path that was expected. Most parents are confused as to what they could have done better to prepare their child for the shift to adulthood.

Today's parents understand that it's harder than ever to get into college, compared to ten to twenty years ago. The headlines of news stories each fall boast the tremendous challenge of being accepted into college for students today. For example, one *New York Times* article began, "Applications to select colleges and universities are reaching new heights this year, promising another season of high rejection rates and dashed hopes for many more students."[2]

As we saw in chapter 3, today's parents experience tremendous anxiety over whether their child will get into a good college, and that worry can set in when children are still very young— even as young as preschool. To keep up with this pace, parents may jump in to help beef up their child's academic résumé with tutors, enrichment classes, and more. Often this results in children being overscheduled and stressed. We interviewed many teachers before writing this book, and they consistently reported that, as a group, students are more apathetic, dependent, and anxious than in years past. All parents want to help their children be prepared for the challenges of higher education, but in fact, the opposite is happening. If it is not a child's GPA, SAT/ACT scores, or the number of AP classes on the transcript that prepares him or her for college, what does?

What the Experts Say Makes a "Successful" Student

We asked teachers across the country to share the characteristics they have found to be the most predictive of a successful student.

There is a very consistent theme of character traits:

- Resiliency or the ability to handle stress
- Internal motivation
- Perseverance and persistence
- Positive social skills, including communication skills
- Independent problem-solving ability or critical thinking
- Willingness to take responsibility

Notice that the teachers did not report IQ, GPA, or "honors student" as being a predictive characteristic. In fact, not one teacher cited a specific score, number, or objective measure. Every teacher emphasized character qualities and skills necessary to deal with life's challenges. One teacher simply said, "Embrace failure and struggle as part of learning."

One Southern California high school teacher reported that she had asked her students what characteristics they saw as most important in peers who are successful. The students' perspective was very similar to the teachers' view. They said being resilient, politely assertive, determined, and dedicated were the most important. They also reported time management, study skills, and social skills are critical for a student to learn to prepare for higher education or a job. Not one student said anything about IQ, GPA, or the ability to take advanced classes.

Not only do teachers and students find character qualities important, but the research also supports this conclusion. A study completed with a group of academically focused middle school students found that self-disciplined adolescents outperformed their more impulsive peers on every academic performance measure.[3] The measures included report card grades, standardized achievement test scores, admission to a competitive high school, and attendance. If the goal is to improve grades, test scores, and acceptance into a choice school, teaching children how to be responsible and confident in their ability to solve problems is a very strong predictor. That makes sense. Children who feel confident in their ability to solve a problem and work toward a goal will feel more comfortable finding answers rather than expecting answers to be provided to them. They will also be more diligent in completing quality work. On the other hand, children who are more impulsive and need the immediate solution to a problem are more likely to wait for others to tell them what to do, get stuck when a task is difficult, and complete unsatisfactory work. This does not bode well for a generation of students that is becoming so accustomed to instant gratification. This was further supported by a study that found that "conscientiousness" (defined as "a person who is organized, self-disciplined, and responsible") was the strongest predictor of both high school and college GPA.[4] Parents who push their kids too fast or rescue them to ensure mistakes don't negatively impact their GPA aren't doing them any favors. In the end, it only undermines the character traits that the experts and research consistently find predict college success.

The teachers we interviewed reported that in this generation, students seem to be less self-disciplined and more eager to have an immediate answer, particularly when it comes to schoolwork. One high school English teacher said, "If it is not *Googleable*, they are lost." He shared an instance when he asked his students for their ideas about a possible connection between two events in literature. He said there was no right or wrong answer and he simply wanted them to "think." Instead, more than half of the class typed his question verbatim into Google on their tablet. It was an automatic reaction to a question about their opinion.

They were unwilling (or unable) to think for themselves and depended on something else to provide the answer. Their need for instant answers is becoming as rampant in education as in other areas of their lives.

While research shows that self-disciplined adolescents out-performed their more impulsive peers on every academic measure, the phenomena of instant gratification, overparenting, and rescuing children contradicts this at every level. Instead, there is an assumption that intelligence is the top predictor of success. Research and our interviews with teachers, administrators, and employers show that is inaccurate.

How Intelligence Is Misunderstood

High school teachers continually told us that AP and honors classes are often thought of as a status symbol. They shared that some parents think it is in their child's best interest to be in advanced courses in high school even if the child has never displayed an advanced ability in the subject or if their schedules don't allow for the extra time needed to do the work. The result is that the student earns a lower grade in the advanced class, when they would most likely have earned a higher grade in the general class. So why is there such a push?

—Dr. Darlene and Dr. Ron

We find it very interesting that the words "intelligence" or "smart" were never used in our interviews with teachers, administrators, and parents as qualities they found most important in an emerging adult. However, they are words that children and parents often use when discussing school aspirations. Parents readily point out the smart kids and assume they are the ones who will be successful in college and life. There are so many assumptions attached to these words.

The term *smart* is commonly used to describe a personal attribute. It is also one of those words imbued with inferred meaning. Students may describe a group of kids as "the smart kids," meaning they get good grades. An adult may describe a coworker's idea as "smart," meaning original or effective. A parent may describe their child as "smart, even though her grades don't show it," meaning it is not based on academic performance. Dictionary.com defines it as "having or showing quick intelligence or ready mental capability."[5] Most people would consider smart to be synonymous with intelligent.

So what is intelligence and how is it measured? In the field of cognitive psychology, this question has been debated for decades. Many theories of intelligence have been developed over the years. Theorists have attempted to identify a single measure of intelligence, multiple abilities that interact to make up an overall intelligence, multiple types of different intelligences, and emotional intelligence.[6] When someone is described as smart, what does that really mean? Is she book smart, street smart, socially smart, all of the above, or something else altogether?

Whatever the outcome of the intelligence debate, children clearly hear the message that it is good to be smart, and kids who get good grades are the smart kids. Children regularly tell us that the smart kids are the ones who don't have to study, and that school is easy for them. Following this logic, does this mean that if a child encounters a challenge, he is *not* smart? Kids are sure getting that message.

Not only is this a detrimental message to convey to children, but it plays right into the Instant Gratification Generation.

If a student has to study a lot to earn an A on a test, he is not described as one of the smart kids. This is a great example of how getting something easily, not waiting or working for it, is unintentionally rewarded. Getting the good grade is praised, rather than working hard for the grade.

Not only does the notion that "easy equals smart" support the desire for instant gratification, but it also contradicts the core ideas of executive functioning. Working hard for a good grade requires planning, initiative, motivation, and perseverance, which are all important components of executive functioning. Because the Instant Gratification Generation is so vulnerable to falling into the traps of ease and convenience, equating smart with having things come easily fits right into their perception. Unfortunately, this is an inaccurate and misleading perception.

Don't Associate Grades with Intelligence

We have worked with many teens who were described as smart through elementary school because they were early readers or because math came easily to them. Once they reached middle school, managing the increased workload became more difficult. Not only were they asked to learn material, but they needed to organize longer projects, manage multiple subjects, and study for more comprehensive tests. They were required to use skills they never needed to practice before when the academics came so easily. Put simply, school came so easily when they were young that they never learned how to be a good student.

For academically advanced students, praise the

work they put toward a project or test and refrain from associating their grades with how smart they are. Here are some examples:

- "Johnny, you have been studying for a long time. That really shows perseverance."
- "Jane, I am really proud of you for starting that project early."
- "You really earned that A because you worked hard, took your time to do your best work, and learned the information too."
- "We are OK with a C on that test because we know how hard you studied and prepared. Maybe you can learn from how you studied this time to better prepare for the next test."

Emphasize the Process of Learning

As we discussed in chapter 3, it is difficult for parents to resist stressing over the objective markers that assess their child's achievements—including reading level, test grades, standardized test scores, and number of advanced placement classes on the transcript. Yet those metrics are all *end products*. The effort, initiative, planning, problem solving, and the organization that it takes to meet goals are the *process*. These are the skills and abilities required to complete a task or learn. End products are clear and objective, and it seems easy to identify a child's level of accomplishment just by examining them. It's much more difficult to assess a child's planning, organization, initiative, and other learning skills in general, because those take time and effort to achieve. Children can become frustrated, discouraged, and anxious as they are learning these skills, especially if it doesn't look like they are being successful. Indeed, when they talk about the smart kids in their class, they often tell the story with a sense of admiration and awe. For parents, it feels more comfortable to say, "My child is in the advanced math class" than, "My child set up a meeting with her teacher after school to find out how to bring her grade up after she missed an assignment." Yet the communication skills, planning, and initiative it takes to set up the meeting and do the extra work are very important life skills that will benefit her long after completing that single class. They also show the character traits experts found to be so important in predicting later success.

It is great to feel proud of children for an achievement measured by an objective marker, like getting an A on a test. However, it is the overarching assumptions that are made based on those markers that can negatively impact a child's view of himself or herself. For example, the State of California has a Gifted and Talented Education (GATE) program. If students score above a certain point on a single qualification test, they are classified in GATE and, depending on the school district, they can be offered higher level work. These students take only a single visual problem-solving test to qualify for GATE. In other words, a single score on one test leads to many assumptions on the part of parents, teachers, and students alike. It is assumed that students with this designation are brighter, more advanced, and more able to do more challenging work than their peers—but really, this test simply identifies visual problem solvers. Conversely, other gifted students who are not visual problem solvers (e.g., verbal or auditory learners) do not receive this designation. As a result, students are not encouraged to discover and capitalize on their different learning styles—instead they hear the message that they are not one of the smart kids. These students then learn it is the objective measure that defines their intelligence. It is really important that parents don't reinforce these messages in their interactions with their children. Instead, parents should explain to their children what each single score measures. For example, "The kids who are in the GATE program are really good at solving visual puzzles," or "The kids in that program happen to have really good math skills."

Reward Progress

When discussing grades, reward and praise "positive" grades instead of "good" grades. If a child is a strong math student, an A is a positive grade. On the other hand, if math is a real challenge, a B might be a positive grade if he or she put forth a lot of effort. If a student begins the year with C grades on projects or tests because the teacher is very detail oriented and docks points for each little mistake, then earning a B is a positive grade.

Elementary School

When our son was in first grade, I volunteered in the Morning Read program. For the first twenty minutes of class each day, the students would read out loud to a parent volunteer and then answer questions about what they read. I noticed that our son was only one of three students who was not reading a chapter book. His teacher shared with me that having so many students reading at an advanced level was unusual, but becoming more common. She said that she did not feel it was for the best and that these students may be reading the words in the books above their grade level, but most of them did not understand what they were reading. She shared that it is much more important to read books with information the students can understand, even if they have the ability to read more difficult words.

—Dr. Darlene

We hear this same sentiment from teachers all the time. Another first grade teacher shared that she continually needs to talk with parents about sending in reading material that their children can remember and comprehend, rather than the high-level books they were bringing to class. She said that parents are so proud their children are reading books above grade level that they didn't consider the fact that they missed the more essential practice of learning how to integrate and understand what they read.

Reading comprehension is a problem-solving task that requires children to integrate the facts, relate them to things they already know, analyze the accuracy, remember what they read, and be able to discuss the information. Reading books that are developmentally appropriate allows children to practice those essential thinking skills—even if that means the book is "easier." If parents push the more difficult book because of the implication that their child is considered more advanced, the child will struggle with comprehension and can't practice the problem solving that goes with reading.

The same concept holds true in math. The student who completes simple math facts the fastest is deemed the smartest

in math. Whereas, some students might think about the principles underlying the math facts as they complete them, which
slows them down. They are exercising strong thinking skills,
but not getting the same label of "smart." Whether it is GATE
designation, reading level, or how quickly a student completes
math problems, elementary school is full of instances where an
objective measure begins to define how students see themselves.

Starting early on in elementary school, both parents and
students are drawn to make comparisons between objective
academic measures, and sometimes that can lead to feelings of
insecurity in your child if she's not doing as well as her peers.
The comparisons will happen, but you can guide how your child
interprets the differences in many ways.

Make Explanations Meaningful for Your Child

Some children work very hard and earn lower grades
than their effort would indicate. This can be discour-
aging and make them feel less capable than their
peers. When talking with children about their academic
strengths and weaknesses, it is helpful to give specific
examples that make sense to them.

Here is one explanation: "What grade a student gets
does not indicate how smart they are; it just shows how
they are doing in that class. If a kid gets an A in math,
they aren't smarter than everyone else; they are just
good at math. If a student gets an A in history, they aren't
smarter than everyone else; they are just good at history. If a student is the captain of the football team, they

aren't smarter than everyone else; they are just good at football. So the kids that are getting an A in biology aren't smarter than you. Biology just makes more sense to them."

Middle School

When children transition into middle school, it can be challenging to learn how to organize multiple classes and different teacher expectations for the very first time. This is also a time when parents communicate with the teacher less and students are expected to manage the work on their own. How parents help their children navigate these years makes a strong impact on teaching their children to think and solve problems.

Remember, this is the time a child's brain is primed to take on these developmentally appropriate challenges, such as the executive-functioning skills discussed in chapter 5. Inevitably, students are going to stumble their way through the first months (or years) of middle school. This is to be expected. We like to call middle school the "practice years." It is harder for parents to look over their shoulders and we see that as a very positive thing. This is an opportunity for the student to make mistakes, figure things out, and do things differently before entering high school.

It was the second month of our son's sixth-grade year and he told us he had a unit test the next day. Our conversation went like this:

"Did you study?"

"No. I know everything."

"Really? Three chapters, all of your notes, and the list of vocabulary words?"

"Yep."

"Hmmmm. OK. You get one try to see if this no study-ing thing works."

Three days later, he came home looking sheepish and told us he needed us to sign his test to show that we saw it. He earned an F. Our response was, "Well, now you know that didn't work. You don't get to take that approach again."

—Dr. Darlene and Dr. Ron

We could have told him that he needed to study and that if he did not earn a good grade he would be grounded, but he truly thought his method would work, and we wanted to give him the opportunity to learn from his decisions. If he studied because we made him, he would never learn what it took to get the grade he wanted. It also would have risked beginning a pattern of us, as parents, being in charge of his planning. That is the beauty of the "practice years." Yes, he earned an F and it really brought down his overall grade. But in middle school, the long-term effect was minimal and the experience was much further reaching. A middle school counselor we speak with frequently tells parents, "If you take the responsibility, she (he) doesn't have to—and won't."

Middle school is also a time when students can get really behind and overwhelmed with all the changes and expectations. Parents can support them in figuring things out by providing very structured and consistent guidance in navigating websites, using a planner, establishing a homework routine, and so on. These are new productivity and time-management skills that, for most students, need to be taught (and will of course benefit them later in life when they transition to the workplace).

While many students will need guidance to initially learn the skills and most are going to make mistakes, they should not be rescued. Parents will know if they are rescuing their child rather than guiding them if they do any of the following things:

- Call teachers on their child's behalf. Instead, middle school students should send the email or talk with the teacher before the parents intervene.
- Make excuses to teachers about why their child missed an assignment.
- Contact the teacher to find out how to raise their child's grade (the student should inquire if there are options).
- Bring forgotten assignments to the student at school.
- Take their child's perspective (or story) without considering the teacher's side. For example, if the student tells the parent how unfair something is and the parent automatically agrees with the child.
- Call the school to change their child's schedule or try to get a different teacher.
- Go to the principal about a matter without first talking with the teacher.
- Complain about teachers within earshot of the student.

Almost every teacher we spoke with said that their biggest challenge is when a parent agrees with and encourages a student's criticism of a teacher without giving that person the benefit of the doubt or getting all the information first. This is especially true because a child's recitation of a scenario is likely to be biased in his or her own favor.

How a parent approaches these challenging years can set up patterns for how their children take on the responsibility of school and jobs. Let's look at a scenario that illustrates the difference in lessons learned.

> Nick, a middle school student, has a teacher who is a little disorganized, so she sometimes loses homework and does not always update her website. Nick is earning a C in the class and when his parents look at the grade book online, they see that there are several missing assignments. Nick tells them that he finished one of the assignments and doesn't know why there is a zero. He said he didn't know he was supposed to do the others because his teacher did not put them on her website. He proceeds to tell his parents that she is really disorganized and all the kids are missing assignments because of this.

Option 1

Nick's parents become upset with the teacher, send her an email, and complain to each other about her lack of organization. If they did this, the teacher would likely reply that she made a mistake and neglected to enter the grade for one assignment, but would give Nick credit. She would also acknowledge that she is not great at keeping her website up to date, but that she always tells the students the assignments in class. She may even give Nick the option of making up the missed assignments. This would result in an improved grade, Nick would feel relieved, and the parents would feel satisfied that the problem was resolved.

At the same time, this solution would teach Nick nothing about solving the problem on his own. In fact, it would give him an excuse for not writing down the assignment the teacher gave in class, because he could rely on the convenience of her website. He wouldn't have to think about how to solve the problem and by telling his parents about it, he could get an immediate solution by letting them solve it.

Option 2

Nick's parents say to him, "You were responsible for keeping track of these assignments and you didn't do them. These zeroes affected your grade, which means no time with friends until you bring your grade up." When Nick responds with shock, saying it is unfair because missing the assignments was not his fault, his parents tell him, "OK. If you think it was unfair, what are you going to do?" Nick talks to his teacher and gets credit for the mistakenly missed assignment. She reminds him that she always tells the students the assignments in class (maybe gives him the option of making up the missed assignments), and he learns that for this teacher, he can't depend on the website. Going forward, Nick writes assignments down in his homework planner. This teaches him problem solving, conflict resolution, communication, planning, organization, self-esteem, and confidence.

Avoid the Rescue and Reinforce Practice

If a student has a middle school teacher whose expectations seem unreasonable (or are unreasonable), take the opportunity to teach the student to deal with it in mature and appropriate ways. First, identify whether the teacher is acting in a demeaning, hurtful, or otherwise, harmful manner. If so, it is time to jump in and stand up for your child. If not, talk with your child about how to approach the situation. "What do you think you should do?" and "How are you going to deal with this?"

- **Step 1:** Make sure the student approaches the teacher to get more information first. If the teacher is receptive, then the student can go ahead and talk with him or her about a plan to address the issue.
- **Step 2:** If the teacher is not receptive, draft an email together with your child, not for your child (a lot of teachers don't listen to voice mail). The email should address the child's understanding of the issue and their role in the problem, as well as the proposed plan to address the problem. It may not be to fix the problem, but should indicate the child's intention to take responsibility. For example, if a child does not get credit for an assignment turned in late, he can complete the assignment to show responsibility even though he won't get credit.
- **Step 3:** If email communication is not productive, a meeting between parent, student, and teacher may be needed.
- **Step 4:** If the meeting is unsuccessful and there is indeed a poor fit between the student and teacher, discuss ways to "get through it" in the most responsible and respectful way possible. Then offer a lot of praise to the student about their effort toward dealing with this tough situation and point out the really admirable things the student is doing to get through the semester. Do not conspire with the student and complain about the teacher. Instead, talk about the mismatch between teaching style and the student's preferences. "I get it. You don't like your teacher, but I am really proud of you for taking responsibility for doing your work and doing the best you can."

High School

As a student approaches high school, the anxiety surrounding academic performance skyrockets. To no surprise, we find it is very often the parents who are feeling more anxious than the students when considering (or pushing for) advanced high school classes. The truth is, if a child is ready for the advanced classes, he or she will be encouraged by teachers, excel in entry-level classes, and be excited about the subject. If advanced-level work suits your child's learning style and she thrives in that environment, that's great! But remember that it is not a measure of intelligence or a predictor of whether your child is going to be successful in college. Some students may never be ready for honors or AP-level classes in high school and that is OK too. As we saw in chapter 2, parents should be careful not to pressure their children by treating honors or AP-level coursework as status symbols. Again, it is the emphasis on the product or outcome that deflates a student's affinity toward learning.

High school is also a very vulnerable time for parents to feel the need to jump in and rescue their children. They begin to tell themselves that there are only a few years left and they just need to "get them through." For many, the temptation to rescue is at its highest during these years because "they really count." They think that if they throw in as many last-minute pushes as they can, their child will be more prepared. In fact, it makes them *less* prepared. These rescue attempts undermine the student's effort and take away opportunities for them to build self-confidence in their skills. Students who are more confident in their skills are able to be more excited about and open to taking on the challenges that come with learning new things.

Resist the Temptation to Push Too Fast

A longtime teacher and counselor shared the following advice: "Children should take the most rigorous courses they can take where at the end of the day they can still go to soccer practice or be in the marching band and come home and sit at the table to have a nice family interaction. There has to be balance."

These are wonderful guidelines. It allows for the individual needs of the student as well as includes executive-functioning practice and consideration of others that is essential to teach.

Each child develops at her own pace, so how are parents supposed to know what is developmentally appropriate for their children if they don't compare them to other children? Here are some guidelines to identify if you are pushing your children too fast:

- What does the child say about schoolwork? Is it too easy or hard?
- Does the child become stressed out when talking about school?
- Is the child easily frustrated around schoolwork?
- Is the child complaining of stomachaches or other physical symptoms, especially during the school year?
- Is there a lot of crying around homework?
- Is the child saying he or she is not smart or good at school?

These are all indications that the child is out of his optimal zone for learning and it is time to evaluate where the insecurity is coming from.

Academic Self-Concept

When encouraging children to become excited about learning, it is very important to help them develop a positive academic self-concept. A person's *academic self-concept* is the way he or she identifies with what type of student he or she is. It is how he would describe himself as a student. A person has many different aspects to their overall self-concept and likely identifies with each aspect differently. For example, every person will identify with their athletic, artistic, musical, social, emotional, or academic self-concept in different ways. A person might identify with being "really creative" or "bad at art" when thinking about her artistic self-concept or "really friendly" or "a loner" when thinking about her social self-concept. While there are numerous aspects to a person's self-concept, the academic self-concept tends to be the most ingrained and difficult to change once it is established. When thinking about your own academic self-concept, you are likely to have a quick answer to the question about what type of student you were. Adults will often make comments like, "I was never good at math," "I was always smart in school," "I wasn't a good student," "School was easy," or "Teachers never liked me." Very often, how children see themselves as a student comes from the objective markers we have discussed.

Because school poses multiple challenges for students, it offers many opportunities for parents to help shape the way their children view themselves as students. Students begin to define their academic self-concept early on, usually by comparing themselves to other students. For example, as we saw in the last chapter, if a child is not able to complete math problems as quickly as his or her peers, weekly timed tests can become a source of frustration. If a child is not at one of the top levels in the class, parents may begin to hear "I am not good at math" or "I am not one of the smart kids." How quickly a child can complete a math sheet is in no way indicative of whether he or she is "good at math," but this is the message that the child internalizes. These comparisons happen all the time. Parents can use this opportunity to help reframe the idea that a specific skill does not define their child.

Use Real-Life Examples to Show Success with Challenges

There are many different skills required for each academic area. It is very important for students to understand they can be really good at a subject even if they are not great at one part of it. The Internet is an amazing tool to find famous people who were tremendously successful despite challenges in specific academic areas.

Did you know Jane Austen and Ernest Hemingway were poor spellers? Agatha Christie was dyslexic *and* a tremendously successful writer. And Thomas Edison, an inventor who was called a "wizard," was poor at math.

One of the best ways for parents to help their students have a positive academic self-concept is to focus on their child's achievements as a whole. Achievements are defined not only by the objective measures but also by the effort, consideration, sensitivity, and awareness he brings to his schoolwork. In addition to the tips on helping a child understand that a specific skill does not define a child, there are many amazing personality traits that are there when a child is sensitive to his performance.

> When working with kids who are feeling down about their school performance, I will often say this:
> "The fact that you care about how you are doing shows me so much. It shows me that you are considerate and responsible and hardworking. That is something that not many kids your age think about. It is also something that is really hard to teach. You have those gifts naturally. You have a lot to be proud of and I can't wait until you get past this tough school stuff so you know how much ahead of most kids you are."
>
> —Dr. Darlene

Complaints about Teachers

> A mother shared with me that her daughter was having a difficult time with her first year of high school. She said that most of her daughter's teachers were "good," but that two of her teachers did not keep their website updated with what homework was assigned for the week. She asked me, "What is she supposed to do if she misses a day and doesn't know what work she missed?" I answered, "Do what we all did. Call a friend or talk to her teacher when she returns to come up with a plan for making up the work." In fact, having teachers who gave homework in class rather than posting it on the website might be the best thing that happened

that year. She could take the opportunity to learn how to follow instructions that were provided verbally. She would need to write it down, keep a calendar, and plan her day accordingly. Adapting to different teaching styles in high school is wonderful preparation for learning how to work with different professors and bosses later on.

—Dr. Darlene

It is always a major red flag for us as therapists when we hear parents talk about all the negative experiences their children have had with teachers. We are not talking about a single negative experience, but parents who can recite criticisms for each teacher their child had over the course of multiple years.

We understand that it is desirable for children to have positive experiences with teachers who nurture their strengths and assist them in compensating their weaknesses. However, teachers are individuals with their own personalities. There is no way for every teacher to be a great fit for every student. Just as students have different learning styles, teachers have different teaching styles, and there will be times when a teacher-student match is not perfect. Maybe the teacher's personality is strict and the child prefers nurturance, or maybe the teacher is a stickler for detail and the child feels the grading is unfair. This is not only true for a child's experience throughout school, but it will be true for his experience throughout life. A supervisor's managerial style will not always be to the preference of all her employees.

Throughout this book, we have continually discussed how important it is for children and teens to have the opportunity to practice life skills throughout their childhood. Well, having a teacher who is not a perfect fit is a great opportunity to practice tolerance, patience, and empathy for individual differences. In many ways, learning to work through these issues with teachers might be more important than the letter grade.

When parents are vocal about their disapproval of their child's teachers, it gives their child an excuse to avoid taking responsibility. The child may begin to blame the teacher's grading policies, bias against her, or poor teaching skills as the reason she doesn't do her work. So instead of getting a B (when maybe she deserved an A, which might be unfair), she gets a C, lunch detentions, and/or feels angry throughout the year. Further, since it is easier to blame someone else than take responsibility, this can quickly develop into a pattern. Children have a choice about how they deal with it, and as a parent, you can help them navigate these difficult situations by promoting social skills and problem solving.

Whether a situation is truly unfair or not, parents should never put their child in the victim role. Once a child feels he is the victim, he can stop taking responsibility and he feels that all problems are the fault of someone else. On the other hand, if parents guide their children in coping with the situation, then they get practice dealing with difficult interpersonal situations. Most students will have experiences with teachers who are not well matched, especially when they have up to six teachers per year. People have differences and disagreements are normal. We encourage parents to use the experiences as teaching moments.

Stay Positive about the Teacher

Before your child even reaches high school, he will probably have at least twenty different teachers. Therefore, the child is likely to have a few teachers who aren't a great match for his learning style. Instead of suffering through a year of frustration, take the opportunity to help your child overcome the situation and help prepare him for high school, college, and future jobs. The best way to do this is to stay positive about the teacher. Under no circumstance should children hear parents complain about a teacher. As soon as a child thinks you don't like a teacher, he has no choice but to align with you as the parent. This results in reduced motivation and effort in the classroom and a missed chance to practice overcoming challenges. Make the year one of the best for your child.

Parents to the Rescue: Beware of the Common Excuses

As we saw in chapter 1, parents who rescue their children from making mistakes at school are falling into one of the most common traps we encounter as therapists: the rescue trap.

Between our experiences with all the students we work with every day, teachers we interact with weekly, and our own children's excuses, we have extensive firsthand knowledge of the ways children and parents communicate the need to be rescued (sometimes without even realizing it).

What Children Say

- "If you don't do this, I will get a bad grade and it will lower my whole GPA."
- "It is a group project and I am the only one working on it."
- "My teacher didn't post it on the website until yesterday."

- "I had soccer practice so I forgot to check the website."
- "The teacher is really disorganized."
- "Nobody told me it was due tomorrow."

What Parents Say

- "It's just this once."
- "If I don't do it, there will be a lot of drama at home tonight."
- "My child will hate me if I don't."
- "My child was so panicked last night that he or she couldn't finish the project, so I needed to help."
- "His teacher is horrible anyway."

Parents also tell us that it feels good when their child still needs them when they offer some way to save the day. They tell us that they feel involved in their children's lives if they help their children in that way. When parents rescue their kids, there is typically an outpouring of gratitude. Face it, how often does that occur, especially with teens? It is understandable that parents are so easily lured into the trap.

While the trap is tremendously alluring, it is important to remember that teachers consistently reported that this is what interferes with a student's learning the most. It also contradicts all those characteristics that research, teachers, and teenagers themselves reported were indicative of strong and successful students, as we discussed earlier in this chapter.

When asked how parents can best support their children academically, here is what teachers interviewed from across the country said:

- "Allow children to struggle with challenging situations,

coaching rather than solving for them. Hold them account-
able for their actions and follow through with discussions
about how the child would handle the situation better to
achieve a more positive outcome. Love them for who they
are and appreciate their personal strengths and gifts!"

- "Realize that enabling doesn't equal good parenting;
require that the students' speak and deal with the teachers
themselves; encourage them to build relationships with
adults who can become mentors, potential references who
would write them a letter of recommendation or future
networking connections."
- "Encourage them to foster their own passions and teach
them that success doesn't come from being 'smart,' 'gifted,'
'athletic,' and so on, but through hard work, perseverance,
and grit."
- "Encourage independent thinkers by asking questions
instead of doing things for their kids."
- "Allow them to struggle to develop solutions on their own."
- "Not only can parents help their kids when their students
are 'stuck' on their math homework, but they can allow
kids to problem solve around the house rather than do
everything for them."
- "Read, read, read."
- "You can't smother them and do the work for them. They
need the chance to struggle, and fail. Don't bail them out,
but give them the support when necessary."
- "Place value on literacy by as regularly as possible setting
time aside where all family members read."
- "The most important thing parents can do is be involved
with their child's education—know who their teachers are,
what they're studying/learning, and so on—without being

helicopter parents. Parents need to foster independence in their kids."

- "I believe in the expectations and modeling of work ethic, organization, attention to detail, and so on.

- "A parent's role is to sometimes be the 'bad guy' and to not always give in to their child, just as a teacher's role is to educate and reinforce the boundaries of young-adult life."

We did not leave any teacher responses out of these lists nor did we only choose the ones that fit with our perspective. Research, teachers, administrators, and clinicians all agree that the most important skills and abilities to promote in our children are character traits developed through having the opportunity to learn how to solve problems while at the same time being considerate of other people and the consequences of their choices.

Putting It All Together

The Issue

Focusing on the end product is more comfortable for many parents because it is measurable and provides evidence their child is doing well. Parents also don't want their children to be left behind and want to celebrate their strengths, which means they focus on objective measures of their achievements like letter grades and GPA.

The Trap

Parents can get caught up in the "talk" among other parents about the achievements of their kids' peers. This leads them to push their children too fast or focus on the small details, rather than the process of learning (planning, organization, initiating, problem solving, and making and fixing mistakes). When children are denied opportunities to learn, they may get the grades or test scores to be admitted into the college of their choice, but they are lacking the skills to manage life independently once they get there.

The Alternative

Understand that test scores, grades, and academic awards are based more on work effort than intelligence. Point out and reinforce the work they put toward academics. Take note of effort, planning, organization, initiation, and communication about their academic performance.

1. Help your child develop a positive academic self-concept by discussing a balance of strengths and weaknesses. One way to do this is to avoid talking about the smart kids. Instead, talk about the individual gifts of some kids. For example, "Wow, John is really good at math," "Sue is a great reader," or "Matt is really coordinated." Then make sure to point out the gifts of your children.

2. Another way to support a positive academic self-concept is to talk about areas of challenge as individual challenges. It is important not to generalize them to what type of student a person is or how it relates to intelligence.

3. When discussing grades or academic measures, use the phrase "positive grades" (or scores) rather than "good grades." This takes the focus from the number and emphasizes the child's effort.

4. Have your child set his own academic goals (know-ing that they might not align with your own). A good time to do this is when report cards come home. Even young children can do this. When the teacher's evaluation is in front of them, the information is much more meaningful and doesn't seem so forced. After goals are set, feel free to support your child and discuss additional concepts he might have overlooked.

CHAPTER 7

The Phones Might Be Smart, but What about Us?

Parent: Dr. Ron, nothing seems to motivate our son to change his behavior. He continues to be disrespectful of our family rules and he is doing terrible in school. We have put him on restriction and taken away video games and other electronics.

Dr. Ron: I noticed that during our session that afternoon he was holding his phone and kept checking it. I asked him why he still had his phone when I had just heard that he had lost his electronics. His response was, "They let me keep my phone in case there is an emergency. I don't think they understand that I can do everything on it. They can take away everything as long as they let me keep my phone."

A recent national survey indicates that 68 percent of twelve- to thirteen-year-olds (middle schoolers) and 83 percent of fourteen- to seventeen-year-olds (high schoolers) have a cell phone.[1] The study goes on to indicate that cell-phone ownership by children is increasing every year. Another study found that 20 percent of third graders and almost 40 percent of fifth graders have their own cell phone.[2]

The Impact of Cell-Phone Use on Children

With the rampant use of cell phones among children and teens, it is important to understand the impacts that cell phones have on children, both positive and negative. Because cell phones are such a common part of the everyday life for this generation, most people assume that they can only be helpful. However, research shows that cell-phone use can have a negative impact on children's ability to process some information.

It is true—the growing dependence on technology is reducing the opportunity for children and teens to solve problems and, ultimately, *to think*. A recent article previewing a large national study suggests that too much technology takes a toll on kids' ability to utilize working memory.[3] *Working memory* is the ability to hold information in short-term memory while figuring out how to use the information. Because so much data and storage is available with a smartphone, children and teens are not required to remember many things (e.g., phone numbers). Therefore, they are not strengthening this ability. They depend on technology to plan their day and remind them of their responsibilities rather than building an internal ability to do this. Technology is a wonderful tool to assist with time management and planning, but it becomes a hindrance when children and teens rely on it to the exclusion of taking personal responsibility. When they fail to fulfill a commitment because their phone didn't remind them, more and more teens blame the phone rather than taking ownership of the mistake, as if that is an acceptable excuse.

In addition, we are more likely to remember the most recent things we have experienced. A recent conversation or something we read will be stored in our short-term memory until we experience new things that take its place. If a teen is checking his or her phone every few minutes and is texting, using social media, looking at pictures, and checking for email, then these activities will be the things that are retained in the short-term memory. This means that teenagers will not likely remember what you asked them to do right before they began playing with their phone, because they may have a dozen new experiences to cloud their memory in only a few minutes. Good luck getting the trash taken out, the dog fed, or the room cleaned if you ask while a child is playing with his or her smartphone. When children are plugged into their phone, they are disconnected from their environment and everything that is going on around them, which includes being attentive to and remembering your requests, as well as seeing the cues in their environment that remind them what needs to be done.

Separate Homework Time from Phone Time

Smartphones have a lot of useful tools on them that seem like great homework aids. In most circumstances, though, a smartphone shouldn't be part of the process. Children are too often distracted by all the other things they can be doing on the phone instead of homework. It is a lot more fun to check social networks and email or play a game than it is to do homework. It is just simply too tempting for most kids. So be observant and wary if your kids have their phones while doing homework or studying.

How Smartphones Inhibit Problem-Solving Skills

With such a dependence on cell phones, children and teens are losing even more opportunities to learn how to solve dilemmas. As we discuss throughout this book, identifying regular ways for children to practice problem solving is the most important and effective way for them to learn how to tackle the challenges that life throws their way. However, with the dependence on technology—in this case, smartphones—to solve problems for them, they are losing this essential practice.

Consider this scenario: A fifth-grade child is told by her father before school to "wait on the steps in front of school when you are let out today." When 2:30 comes around, classes are dismissed, and the young girl dutifully arrives at the steps to wait for her father to arrive. When she does not see him at 2:30, she impatiently checks her phone and starts calling and texting her father to see why he isn't there. Her dad sends a text saying that he will be late but to continue to wait on the steps at school. Eventually, she is safely picked up with no undue anxiety for any of the parties involved.

However, this scenario also doesn't provide the child with critical-thinking opportunities. Without the phone, she would need to show patience and wait a few minutes, consider the various reasons her father might be late, and then, after some time, figure out what to do—for example, continue waiting, let someone in the school office know her parents hadn't shown up, call a grandparent or neighbor, or even walk home. These are all more difficult choices than looking at a cell phone and retrieving a text with instructions about how to behave. But ultimately, that's the point. This child gets the opportunity to make decisions and solve the problem on her own.

Childhood is a great time to practice thinking and figuring

out problem-solving strategies. Our position is that the child who lacks opportunities to practice these skills will not ultimately develop the skills to the same degree as a child encouraged to come up with possible solutions and pick the best one. We are not saying you shouldn't send your child a text when a plan changes or an unforeseen circumstance occurs. Communication seems like the reasonable thing to do. What we are suggesting is that you try not to become too dependent on rescuing your children from the opportunity to at least *think* about what they might do by providing them with options.

Talk about Your Texts

Cell phones provide a convenient way to communicate with your children, particularly when there is an unexpected change in plans. However, we really encourage you to use each opportunity to talk with your children about what they would do if they did not receive a message or text from you about the change.

Let's take the example of the child who was picked up late from school. If you find yourself in a similar situation, your child's safety and peace of mind are paramount; therefore, go ahead and send the text and then pick up your child as planned. Afterward, have a conversation about what your child might have done if he or she had forgotten his or her phone at home that day (e.g., notify the school office, ask a teacher for help). Let your child take the lead; don't give him or her the answers. This is a great opportunity to see your child think through a situation. Based on what you learn, you can then plan some opportunities to practice safe decision making.

The cell phone isn't the problem. It is how quickly and easily a child can take care of a problem without having to think. Information can be instantly accessed, so there is very little time left for him to consider anything at all. This technologically dependent generation is developing a strong need for instant gratification. The cell phone meets that need perfectly. Similar to many of you, we love our cell phones and aren't giving them up. This is not a condemnation of our appreciation for technology; it is a reminder that opportunities to solve problems are missed because cell phones make so many things easy.

At 10:40 p.m. on a Saturday, a seventeen-year-old is leaving a friend's house and is about to drive home for the night. When he goes out to his car, he notices that one of the tires seems a bit underinflated but not flat. He calls home and says, "Dad, the car has a tire that looks low." His father responds, "I'll call AAA and be right there."

Calling home in this instance is a great idea, no problem there. The opportunity that is lost is what happens next. In the previous scenario, the teenager's father, not the teenager, called AAA for assistance. The boy lost the opportunity to gain experience talking to the dispatcher and feeling comfortable answering all the questions the dispatcher will ask. There wasn't even a discussion about how low the tire was or how far the drive was. Did he consider spending the night at the friend's house and examining the tire in the daylight or even getting a ride home? Because he had a cell phone, he didn't even have to go back inside his friend's house before there was a repair truck and a parent on the way.

Again, the right thing to do was to make the call home. The missed opportunity was the parent who rescued him so quickly. It would be great to know how the teenager would have handled the situation if a parent wasn't able to pick up the phone. In addition, this was a safe environment for him to practice problem-solving skills. He was in front of a friend's house, and help was available right inside. What a perfect opportunity to have him be more active in the decision process. More important, he would have practiced not only dealing with the underinflated tire but also dealing with an unexpected problem too.

It is invaluable for teens to experience having a problem to solve, feeling a little anxiety about what to do, and focusing on the possible solutions. This gives them a sense of pride, accomplishment, and confidence in dealing with problems in the future. The more times a person does this, the more options for solutions that person has in preparation for the next unexpected problem. From a parent's perspective, that is very comforting. The next time you are tempted to rescue your child from a frustrating inconvenience, sit back and rejoice in the opportunity for learning.

"Getting Lost" Teaches Valuable Skills

Reading a map, writing down directions, and estimating how much time it takes to get somewhere is quickly becoming a thing of the past. Our phones are so powerful that our children may never experience the discomfort of being lost. All you have to do is say, or tap, "go home," and your location shows up on a map and the application asks if you are walking, driving, or riding a bicycle. Just for fun, it will tell you every restaurant, market, retail store, or gas station along your route, how long it will take, and ask if you would prefer a fast or scenic route home.

Now think about the skills that are practiced when teens get lost without the benefit of a smartphone. They need to review their plan or route, retrace their steps, find out where they went wrong, and figure out what to do to get back on track. That means looking around and deciding if it is safe to ask someone walking by or go to a gas station or store to get directions. They also have to figure out what to do about the time that was lost. If they are now running late, how are they going to deal with it responsibly? In addition, it teaches a great lesson in time management and planning for the unexpected, especially if they are on their way to an important appointment. Again, we love the convenience and safety of navigation apps such as Google Maps or built-in GPS navigators, but it is important to note that the use of navigation apps highlights even more ways technology decreases the number of opportunities for this generation of teens to practice problem solving.

Reading a map on your phone is easy, but it's not the same as using a paper map, or relying on your memory. Put a paper map in your child's hands, and she hasn't got a clue what to do with it. You will find this out on your next trip to a place so remote that there is no cell phone service or wireless Internet—and what a great opportunity this is to teach alternative ways to solve certain kinds of problems. Just because children and teens have access to the technology doesn't mean you can't encourage them to practice the old-fashioned way. Doing so is a great way to make up for missed opportunities to practice valuable skills.

Use the Smartphone in Productive Ways

If your child is really into his or her smartphone, have your child use it to do fun and interesting things. For example, when you need or want some information, such as an address, movie time, or interesting fact, instead of looking it up yourself, have your child do it for you and then have him or her share the results. The child gets to use the technology and feels like he or she is being helpful. This enables you to interact with your child and praise your child for his or her use of technology, and everybody learns something. If the family is taking a vacation later that year, you might ask your child (or children) to see if there are any amusement parks or water slides in that town. You can even ask a simple question such as, "After dinner, can you find out what time the hardware store opens tomorrow? I can't seem to figure it out." These tasks involve memory, problem solving, and communication and can bring a family together as a unit working as a team.

Text Messaging

A teenage girl showed me a text she received from her boyfriend:

Boyfriend: i dont think we should c each other anymore c u @ skool k?

—Dr. Darlene

Text messaging is here to stay. Parents ask us all the time about texting. Our favorite question goes something like this: "Is it OK that my child sends ten thousand or twenty thousand texts a month?" As illustrated in the previous example, kids text about everything. They fall in love, break up, announce they are bored, share their social calendars, and declare every thought that comes into their impulsive brains. It has become the preferred form of communication for many, even when sitting right next to the person they are texting.

Here is a scary statistic: it is estimated that one-fourth of all texts by teens are sent during school hours.[4] This means not only are students missing educational experiences at school because they are distracted with texting, but they are also doing it in a place where they can easily speak with their friends rather than text. They don't want to wait until a break or between classes to talk to their friends—they need to communicate an idea or comment immediately. The immediacy of texting is also the reason why it's common to use acronyms and make up short versions of words (e.g., GTG means "got to go"). There were once good reasons to abbreviate in text messages, when text entry was difficult, requiring multiple key presses on a small key pad to generate letters, and messages were limited to 160 characters. But now, with full keyboard and auto-fill options, teens do it because typing the words out all the way simply takes too long. For many reasons, texting meets the needs for instant gratification to which this generation has fallen prey.

There are some definite benefits that come with the ease of getting a simple message to someone. On the other hand, there are several drawbacks to this form of communication.

The Missed Social Cues in a Text Conversation

Interacting with someone and being able to communicate a thought or idea effectively is an essential skill for a developing teen. In fact, in chapter 6, we pointed out that it is one of the skills that teachers reported was most indicative of a successful student. Communicating clearly promotes positive peer, teacher, employer, and parental relationships.

Texting qualifies as communicating. So what's the big deal? It's important to remember that words aren't the only way we communicate with each other. We use and interpret body language, facial expressions, gestures, and posture, as well as tone, pitch, rate, and volume of speech. Every time kids get together, face-to-face, they get to practice the art of communication. Just as we believe that practicing baseball makes you a better baseball player, so too holds the notion that practicing communication makes you a better communicator.

When you talk to someone on the phone, you are still able to use many communication skills. You hear not only the words but also speech patterns and fluency. You will be able to pick up on someone's anger, hesitation, praise, sarcasm, confidence, and flirtations on a phone call. When we speak to someone face-to-face, we can also read or gauge their facial reactions. If you make a comment and people roll their eyes, look angry, or walk away, you get instant nonverbal feedback that your comments weren't well received. Even moderately astute communicators take this as a sign not to continue down that path or topic. The opportunity for nonverbal feedback simply doesn't exist in text messages, or emails for that matter. With a text, it is often difficult—if not impossible—to discern the sender's tone or mood. The consequence is that the author of the text may continue down a line of humor or write something that is considered insulting much longer than if he was looking at the person. This strains relationships and creates undue drama. This form of communicating is minimal at best because it does nothing to develop life skills.

Think back to the teenagers who are texting ten thousand times a month. That is a lot of minimalist interacting. There are a multitude of missed opportunities when you send hundreds of text messages a day, every day.

Most people make statements based on who their audience is. When we talk to people, we can see the audience and make judgments about what kind of communication is appropriate. The language we use, content, context, and level of offensive remarks are usually in tune with the audience. You probably wouldn't say something negative about a girl you dated if her older brother was within earshot. When a text is sent, the assumption is that it will only be read by the intended recipient. However, teens commonly share texts with others, resulting in it being read by an audience. When kids send hundreds of texts a day, rather than speaking directly to people, they simply are not practicing the skill of reading the crowd and responding accordingly.

Encourage Face-to-Face Contact Instead of Texting

Texts are great for certain things, such as getting a quick yes or no answer to a question or simply letting someone know you are running a few minutes late. They can also be helpful to see if someone is available to talk, but many teens can have text "conversations" for hours. It is important to monitor the balance between the amount your child is communicating with friends through text versus phone or face-to-face contact. Encourage your children to do as much talking voice-to-voice to their friends as possible because it provides essential practice. If you see your child texting back and forth with a friend from the neighborhood, suggest that your child invite the friend over or perhaps bike or even walk to the friend's house.

Text Messages Can Be Easily Misunderstood

Girl: Can u tell ur friend not to come 2nite?
Boyfriend: idk
Girl: I just want to see u
(No response)
Girl: r u mad at me?
Boyfriend: no
Girl: r u sure?

There was no response for several hours, despite the girl's many attempts to text him. She came to my office in a panic, wondering if he still liked her or if he was going to break up with her. An hour later, she texted him that he could bring his friend if he wanted and she was sorry. Finally, he texted her and wrote, "chill, what's wrong?" It turned out he went out to dinner with his parents and didn't know she was texting him. She made many assumptions based on his lack of response, all of which were incorrect. When I asked why she didn't call him, she said, "That would be awkward."

—Dr. Darlene

Texting is a cultural phenomenon in our electronic age. Smartphones make it so easy to do that teens often send texts without thinking about it. One study even suggests that texting is so easy that 47 percent of the teens surveyed can do it with their eyes closed.[5] That makes the act of text messaging very vulnerable to the impulsive nature of teenagers.

As therapists, we have seen over and over how texting can cause conflicts between teens because full conversations are occurring through text messages. This is wrought with risks of misinterpretations, impulsive responses, and more brazen comments than if the conversation was happening in person. It may begin as a seemingly innocent conversation, and then one comment gets misinterpreted. Instead of clarifying the comment, the other person impulsively reacts with a snarky response. Because neither person is seeing the facial reactions (which may include hurt, anger, embarrassment, or sadness), they are bolder and less thoughtful with their response, which, in turn, results in another strong reaction, and emotions can escalate based on misunderstandings. Seemingly innocent comments can turn into conflicts and hurt feelings.

Important Discussions Deserve Better

We know children are going to text. Therefore, they are going to need the same guidance about communicating in this way as they do with verbal or written communication.

Within the family, one of the rules should be that important things are said directly to the person, not texted. For instance, texting is not an appropriate way to ask to stay out longer, invite someone over to the house, or ask permission for something. This shows children and teens that it is also not appropriate to text a person to ask for a date or formal event, break up, or discuss personal feelings. It is also not appropriate to text an employer to call in sick or quit a job.

The Final Word on Smartphones

A common conflict that parents face regarding technology is "When do I get my child his or her first cell phone?" The decision of when to get a cell phone and what kind needs to be a family decision, and parents should be encouraged to involve their children in the process. There is a lot of support for parents going through this process. Reliable sources such as ABC News, *USA Today*, and the *Guardian* provide great ideas on how to pick a phone and service plan based on a family's needs and the age of the child.[6] They include discussions about Android phones versus the iPhone; MP3, video chat, and Internet capabilities; and most importantly, phones that enable parents to keep tabs on a child's activity, data usage, and location. Additionally, most of the cellular phone companies offer support for parents based on these same principles.

Once a phone is purchased, the family should have rules in place regarding the phone that are consistent with the values they already hold. When used responsibly, the cell phone or smartphone can be a great addition to the family and enhance communication, thinking, and problem solving rather than reduce those actions.

Putting It All Together

The Issue

Smartphones are amazing devices that can do almost everything we are interested in. The saying "there's an app for that" has never been more true. When it comes to children and teens, these phones meet all their needs: instantaneous answers and responses, constant connection to their peers, status, and intense visual and auditory stimulation. The smartphone has a powerful place in a lot of children's lives.

The Trap

Parents of today's Instant Gratification Generation have insisted that children need a cell phone in case of an emergency. Because of this, they have been giving them to their children at younger and younger ages and they are afraid to take them away. Many kids don't earn the privilege of a cell phone or even help pay for it. To this generation, owning one of these phones is their right, and it is culturally and socially reinforced every day. The ability to reach your child at any time is a powerful incentive, but it goes even further. As parents, we want to make sure our children get invited to parties and social events, have lots of friends, and are tuned in to the latest fad or craze. The cell phone makes us think that they will stay connected and never be excluded.

The Alternative

When you first start thinking about getting your child a cell phone, consider what you want your child to use it for and decide which phone best fits your family's needs.

As discussed previously, a lot of reliable sources provide information to help parents with this process.

Once you decide what phone would be the best fit, discuss ways your child can earn it. Whatever you decide, it is important to involve your child in the process. Your child needs to earn it based on grades, effort, manners, or helpfulness around the house. Remember to make your child work for it.

When your child has the phone, it is important to set clear limits and expectations about usage. Parents need to specifically discuss with their children what appropriate usage of the device is and what is unacceptable. There should also be family rules in place about when and how long it can be used.

After all these things are in place, your child is in a position to enjoy his or her smartphone or cell phone in the ways that keep your child safe and let him or her have fun with friends. Stress positive interactions with friends, not lazy interactions. Whenever possible, give your child opportunities to use his or her phone to be helpful or to learn something important and share it with the family. It is always a great idea to model these behaviors for your child when you use your phone.

CHAPTER 8
The Trouble with Technology
Video Games, Social Networking, and Television

A couple came into the office concerned about the amount of time their nine-year-old son was spending playing video games. Once I got more details I realized it wasn't only the amount of time he was playing, but how disconnected he became when playing. His parents said he could lose track of hours without even being aware of it, and when they tried to talk to him, he couldn't pull away.

—Dr. Darlene

Electronic devices are infused into children's lives more than ever before, and it is often to the detriment of interpersonal interaction. When children have unstructured time, their immediate response is to fill that time by using an electronic device. We see it all the time—children in shopping carts, riding in cars, and waiting for a table at a restaurant are interacting with a handheld video game, a smartphone, or tablet to pass the time.

Kids today simply can't wait without being distracted. Electronics suit the Instant Gratification Generation's lifestyle

perfectly because they provide instantaneous and very stimulating feedback. One downside is that there is a total lack of
conventional communication with another person. When they
are focused on the electronic device they are not making eye
contact, engaged in discussion, or connecting to others.

Video Games

Parents often tell us they allow their kids to play video games,
because it's a way to give kids "downtime" and encourage independent play. Indeed, video games are one of the most common
topics about which parents ask us. Should kids be allowed to play
first-person-shooter games? Is online gaming safe? What are
reasonable limits and how much is too much? Research suggests
that today's kids spend almost twice as much time playing video
games as they do reading.[1]

To be honest, there are no great broad sweeping answers to
these questions, but in the following section we will try to put
many of the most important issues into perspective, including
how much is too much, what types of games are okay to play,
and what to do about online gaming. The guidelines we give are
all about balance. The following example is the plan one family
developed to provide balance for their children.

*A family I work with came up with a creative approach
to deciding how much time their sons could play video
games. They call it "Level Up," and it is a form of goal
setting. The kids set their own goals in each video game
in terms of levels, accomplishments, or ranks that they
hope to reach, and they set a time limit to achieve results.
They earn gaming time by meeting their goals and must
stop when they are unable to "Level Up" in a reasonable*

amount of time. It takes video games to a different level when they are being played with a purpose rather than as an escape. What a great way to teach kids how to set reasonable goals and reap the benefits for meeting them. Plus, it relates their interaction with the electronic device back to social accountability. I love it when families come up with creative ways to teach a lesson through a fun activity like video game playing.

—Dr. Ron

How Much Is Too Much?

When parents ask us about an appropriate amount of time for video games, the first issue we consider is often use of time: "What would the child be doing if she weren't playing video games?" As you might imagine, if the neighborhood kids are in their driveways shooting baskets or at a nearby park kicking a ball around, then we think in most instances children are better served being physically and socially active. Unstructured play with friends provides many different chances to practice their social skills. Missing an opportunity to practice every now and then isn't problematic, but when it becomes the standard, there is potential for difficulties down the road. One lesson we learned in chapter 5 was that if children don't routinely practice these skills, they lose them and fail to develop executive functioning.

When the video games are an escape from the pressure of interacting with others, it can become a problem. Video games are especially attractive to kids who struggle with social skills and "playing" with other kids their age. We find that kids with this anxiety are particularly drawn to video games, because that electronic environment imposes almost no social demands and they feel a sense of relief. While video games enable children to feel a temporary reprieve, it can be the start of a vicious cycle where alienation from the social demands of being with peers is relieved by isolating oneself through game playing. That sense of escapism can be very rewarding and perpetuate the cycle of it happening again and again.

Video games also engage children in a manner that is very stimulating and difficult to walk away from, especially if they are a bit uncomfortable interacting with their peers. For some kids it feels really good to tune everything out for a few hours. Take, for example, children who are shy and struggle in school. The six or seven hours a day they are in school are filled with anxiety and hard work, so an opportunity to escape is very enticing. For other kids, the action, sound, and pace of the game is very stimulating and exciting. In both instances kids can become resistant to leaving the game. Parents will know it has become a problem when their child becomes so consumed in the game that he reacts with anger and outbursts when asked to stop playing. These types of reactions are a huge red flag that the child is out of touch with his social environment and adult intervention is required.

Kids in this generation are so programmed for instant gratification that they can't delay progress to the next stage of the game until the next day, and some games lack a pause button that would at least allow them to delay their progress. They want it *now* and can panic if they aren't allowed to keep going. In addition, this pattern is worrisome because not only are they consumed by instant gratification, but they are also not able to deal with the boundaries around video game playing. Playing games as a way of winding down or relaxing is one thing, but playing to frequently escape from the demands of life is concerning. Parents will know it is time to impose structured rules and limits around video game playing when their child:

- can't stop playing when asked,
- becomes so consumed with the game that he or she doesn't react when spoken to, and/or
- leaves the game in an agitated state.

An equally important issue to address when considering how much is too much is the social context of the electronic world of gaming (i.e., "Who else is playing?"). Is there a big group of kids getting together to play and have a tournament? Are kids coming over to the house to play with your child? Are they playing online with friends from school? Does the game put the child in touch with or expose her to total strangers from around the world? These are the kinds of questions that help us gather information on which to formulate feedback for parents. In our neighborhood, there have been occasions where ten to fifteen kids would meet in someone's garage for a tournament. One night they had four TVs linked together and sixteen kids split into two teams were simultaneously playing a single game against each other. That seems like a great use of video games because it promoted face-to-face interaction and prevents the children from losing touch with the world outside their video game world.

Video games can be used as a way to practice interacting and communicating. We believe in *practice*. Playing video games alone as an escape does not provide practice. However, playing video games together with a friend can. For kids who feel social anxiety, expecting them to join ten other kids in a neighbor's garage might be asking too much, but having a single friend over to the house to play video games together and eat chocolate chip cookies might meet the needs of the child and the parent. Who doesn't want to practice eating cookies with a friend? When the video games are "what" the kids are playing together, the situation is similar to playing anything else with friends. The video game serves as an electronic version of a board game. Only when the video game makes the child lose sight of his interactions with other kids does this type of play become counterproductive.

Make Video Games Social

If you believe your son or daughter spends too much time playing video games in isolation, there are several things you can do.

- Set limits on video game playing time (days of the week and number of hours per day), but make it possible for your child to earn more time through things like good grades, great attitude, being social, spending time with the family, or volunteer activities. Whatever your family would like to emphasize is fine. This encourages the activities you want them to do, while decreasing the fighting about the time you set because they can earn more. Begin with a limited amount of time and increase to a level that you think is reasonable.
- Require your child to invite kids over to your home in order to play side by side. This reinforces positive attributes like planning, organization, social skills, and communication. The idea here is to make the playing of video games a social event, not an escape from people and responsibilities.

Set up the electronic equipment in a central and

open location like a family room. The idea here is to keep your child and her video game playing out of her room and other spaces where she can close the door and shut herself off from other people. The amount of violence, adult language, and social isolation tends to increase behind closed doors. Observe what your children and their friends are playing and what happens during the games. It is even possible that simply having you around while they play will annoy them so much that the amount of time they spend on video games will decrease.

Online Gaming

Another important factor to consider with video games is the possibility of online friendships. Some online games involve large groups of people from all over the world coming together to play a single game or to form teams to compete against other teams, known as "massively multiplayer online games" (MMOGs). It is common to make friends with some of these online gamers, especially if they like to play the same games. A child sitting alone in front of a television or video screen may actually be interacting through a headset and microphone with dozens of people from around the globe.

Coming from a generation where no such thing existed (we did have pen pals), it is hard for most parents to equate an online friend with a "real" friend. In many ways, technology makes it easy to avoid the complexity of the real world. However, practicing social skills with a friend via an online video game might actually be providing practice with communication, negotiation, and planning, which are skills that can be transferred to in-person social interactions. A recent study conducted by Hilary

Buff Greenwood found that for the kids who struggle making and maintaining friends the old-fashioned way, having online friends provides a great deal of self-esteem and normalcy for them.[2] Her results remind us that simply being able to say you have a friend—even an online friend—is better than the alternative. Every child benefits from a best friend, and if it's difficult for him to make one in person, having one online can lend comfort and a sense of being normal.

What really is a best friend? At its simplest, a best friend is someone you really like to spend time with who has interests similar to yours. If a video game can open up avenues for a socially anxious child to interact online with others and practice some aspect of social skills, it can be a useful tool.

Remember, when we provide guidelines to parents, it is about balance. The same holds true for online friendships. Parents need to be very aware that video gaming does not replace real-life interactions with people. Instead, online friendships should be seen as initial practice to making friends. Then it can be a comfortable way to maintain social connections for small periods of time, but with a move toward more in-person interactions.

Closely Monitor Online Friends

It is never too early to talk to children about being safe online. With as much time as kids spend on the Internet, it is likely that they are going to make new "friends" there. We also know that not everyone your children might meet online is who they say they are. As a parent, it is important to check in with your children and ask them about their web-based friendships frequently.

- Review your family rules about sharing information online and find out what personal information they have shared. The only information kids should share would be first name (many kids just use a gamer name), and general place of residence (Southern California, New York, Italy, etc.). They need to know never to give a last name, address, phone number, or places they go to hang out.
- Ask them how they "met" their new online friends, what they know about them, and how they learned that information.
- We suggest reviewing your child's online profile and any images she may have posted. It's best to let your kids know you could be looking at any time. If anything seems suspicious or out of the ordinary, you need to investigate further to determine if your child can continue to be "friends" with the individual. The Entertainment Software Rating Board (ESRB) publishes a brochure for concerned parents on their website at www.esrb.cog that is very useful.

One way to check out your children's "friends" is to make it a rule that you are able to listen in on their video game through the headphones—anytime you feel it is necessary. You should not say anything, but just be a silent observer. This should be enough to remind your child that you are taking his online presence seriously, for his own safety, and confirm for you that he understands the family rules and is acting appropriately.

What Type of Video Games Can They Play?

When deciding the limitations around the appropriate uses of video games for your children, it is important to consider the type of video games they are playing. A whole range of games now promotes fitness and keeping kids moving—for example, *Wii Sports* and *Just Dance Kids 2* on the Xbox Kinect. Those interactive games are better than the sedentary types where you bury your body in a beanbag chair to play. In fact, it's pretty satisfying to watch kids actually work up a sweat playing video games.

When choosing what type of video games you allow your child to play, you should always consider the rating, issued by the ESRB. Their ratings guide can be found on www.esrb.org /ratings/ratings_guide.jsp. We could write an entire book about video game ratings, but the fact is, it is a parental decision and each family needs to consider their own boundaries. Children simply want to play whatever their friends are playing without any consideration of the content or appropriateness. There are some red flags to watch out for that will help guide your decisions.

First, video game ratings are there for a reason. Even if your child tells you that an "M" (Mature) rated game is really OK, you need to trust the rating. Also, just because they tell you that "all their friends are playing them" doesn't mean that it is appropriate for your kids, and "all" may turn out to be just two friends. One example of this could be the military or war-simulation games like the *Call of Duty* franchise, which feature realistic weapons, unlimited violence, blood, and gore, and unchecked profanity.

Every child is an individual. It is important to watch for an increase in acting-out behavior that you can closely associate with the content of a video game. Some children simply can't control the adrenaline released when they are playing the more aggressive games. For many kids, it is not that they will imitate things they see, but parents will notice that after playing games with aggressive content, their kids will be more impulsive, aggressive, or verbally inappropriate in person.

Set Limits with Video Games

Like most things in life, a little bit of video game playing probably shouldn't be a big concern to parents. Too much is another story. We recommend the following tips to help you set reasonable limits.

- **Set Priorities:** Video game playing should come after homework and other responsibilities are completed.
- **Watch the Clock:** Set a firm time limit on the number of hours that can be played. Gaming on school days and nights should be minimal, if at all; more on the weekends is probably just fine. Make sure everyone knows what the limits are. Some kids can play thirty minutes a day and they work for that reward. However, if you have a child who is resistant to getting off when the time comes, limiting video games to only the weekend is better.
- **Choose Wisely:** Specifically tell your children which games they can play and which ones are off-limits, even if "everyone else is playing." This discussion should include the consequences of not observing the limits.

If a child thinks he or she needs to hide video game play from you, there is probably a good reason for it. Video games should be played in open space, not behind closed doors. There should be no need for privacy when it comes to playing these games and it will allow you to monitor your child's reaction to the game, as well as how he or she is interacting with other players (whether in-person or virtual).

Social Networking

Websites and social media applications like Facebook, Twitter, Instagram, Tumblr, Snapchat, Pinterest, and whatever comes next make it easy to interact with people via the Internet. You may think this only applies to teenagers, but a recent study found 90 percent of third graders are already online, which means even very young children are at risk here too.[3]

People have their own ideas about how to use these social sites and what rules apply. If you survey your friends and family about how they utilize social networking, you will get as many answers as people you ask. The use of social media ranges from keeping up with friends and family to career networking, and all the way to celebrity stalking. In their simplest form, social networking sites are a lot of fun and a great way to keep in touch with people, and even communicate information like party invitations or special announcements. But social media also makes it very easy for children and teens to feed their need for instant gratification, while potentially putting themselves at risk for identify theft and worse.

Who Is a "Friend" on Social Networking Sites?

Many teens and young adults use social networking sites to monitor the activities of their friends (and compare them to their own), communicate their daily feelings, showcase their activities to other people, and gain new friends. In many ways, it becomes a measure of their social and emotional status, on par with GPA being used to measure smarts, as discussed in chapter 6. However, this is a very misleading communication tool.

Posts on social networking sites are detached from reality. Updates or photos often don't realistically show how a person is doing, just how the person wants others to think she is doing. In that way, a person's profile and activity on a social network is like a reality TV show—she may be a real person, but what she is doing and saying is a performance for the audience. If she sees a peer's post about going to a party, she feels she is not as well liked if she didn't get invited to the party. We continuously hear things like, "Everyone was invited to the party but me," when, in fact, only three of the person's peers got together. It just *seems* like "everyone" when it is broadcast on the social network that she is plugged into. Getting information in this way makes it easy for the Instant Gratification Generation to quickly jump to unfounded conclusions without having much evidence or an opportunity to talk and ask questions about the situation. Very similar to text messages, there is a strong chance for misinterpretation when answers are expected immediately, and the recipient acts, responds, or formulates an emotion without waiting for all the information.

Another misleading piece of information on social media sites is the number of friends or followers a person has on his page. When a teen talks with us about a friend she met on a social networking site, very often the other person is not a friend at all, but someone who was a friend of a friend of a friend, who knew someone the teen actually knows. Yet she is having conversations with these people.

Child: Hey, that kid is one of my Facebook friends.
Parent: Do you want to go say hi?
Child: No, we are not really friends and I don't know him; we are just Facebook friends.

So the concept of a friend has been blurred into an acquaintance or just a name we see on a computer screen.

Gaining a large number of friends and followers has become very important with this generation, particularly because it serves as a status symbol. They want to appear to have a lot of friends online, which those connected to the network associate with being socially popular in person. Another reason is that the more people with whom they are connected, the more things they have to look at to immediately fill their unstructured time. Because of the broad reach to large groups of friends, it is easy to get feedback from a lot of people quickly when you make a post. If a person posts a picture or updates his status on Facebook, he constantly checks to see who might have commented or "liked" it. If he doesn't get the feedback he wants, it impacts his sense of social acceptance. For example, a teen girl shared, "I posted twice and Jan never commented, so I think she is mad at me." She never thought to call Jan and ask her directly, or talk to Jan in person. Instead, the teen was drawing conclusions in real life based on the detached and misleading information provided on the electronic social networking site. She responded impulsively to what she thought should have happened and made instant assumptions when a friend didn't immediately respond. This pattern of allowing an online social network to govern off-line life is becoming very prevalent. This habitual connection to the electronic world really eases children into becoming more comfortable being out of touch.

Social Networking with a Purpose

If your child is becoming dependent on social networking for a large part of her interactions with people, then you need to find a way to limit the amount of time she spends online. Social networking is a great way to set up a meeting time or place or to keep yourself in tune with what your friends are up to. When it becomes a crutch or the foundation for relationships, we suggest guiding your children away from this medium. It probably only takes ten or fifteen minutes a day to check all your networking sites, so consider fifteen minutes per day as a reasonable starting point for how much time to allow your child to engage in online social networking. Consider having your child earn social networking time on his phone or computer by participating in activities with people off-line. That way you achieve the balance between in-person interactions and online ones.

There Is No Privacy in Social Networking

Social networking fits nicely in the comfort zone of most children; it is electronic, stimulating, immediate, and easy. They also like that you don't actually have to talk to people, be groomed or dressed, or even get off the couch to do it. The concern is that things can happen quickly, and impulsive responses and posts happen all the time. Once something is posted, it is there forever, potentially. Even if you go back on the site and remove it, there is no way to control who saw it and what they did with it (e.g., take a screenshot). When celebrities make a post or comment that is extremely insensitive, it is quickly taken down when their agent sees it. However, it is always too late. Once it's posted, it's out there and out of their control. The same thing happens all the time with children and teens. They use social networking sites to express their impulsive emotional reactions to something they experienced. Look at this post from a fourteen-year-old client:

> "To all you who pretend to be my friend: if you can't be a real friend, and you know who you are, you should delete me as a friend because if you don't, I'm going to do it to you anyway!"

That night this girl got texts from two of her friends asking her if she was OK and telling her they were true friends. However, she also went to school the next day and said people avoided her and some gave nasty looks. She posted this after something occurred with two people, but her four hundred online friends and the friends of theirs all read it. This is but one example; we could add many more just like it. A lot of children and teens today simply cannot delay their impulses long enough to think about the appropriateness of their post before putting it out there for everyone to see. They simply do not realize how far reaching their posts can be.

Not only do peers they don't know see their posts, but there are many other people out there collecting information about everyone. Advertisers are looking at your posts to determine what they should be trying to sell you. Employers are looking at your posts to see if you are trustworthy and professional. The social network itself is collecting all your pictures just in case they might want to use them, and they don't need your permission or approval to do so.[4] Most disconcerting, however, is that there are criminals and voyeurs online looking to see if you have made yourself vulnerable in any way that they might be able to exploit. It is important to teach your children to think about what they post, and where, before they do it.

You Should Try It Too

When you think it is time for your child to have their first social networking site, there are some things you should consider doing:

- If your child is on a social networking site like Instagram, Twitter, Tumblr, or Facebook, you should be too. This way you can be familiar with the site and learn about how it is utilized. In this case, ignorance is not bliss.
- With children of all ages, you should set up the account together and make sure you have the username and password, as well as administrative access. You should check regularly to make sure the password has not been changed or updated. With these two pieces of information, you can gain access to the entire account.
- Kids don't need parental permission to register for social networking sites. They simply have to check a box that says they are of age. It is very important for parents to stay up to date, so they know where to look and what to ask their kids about.
- Initially, choose the most restrictive security levels that are offered. These are great safeguards that regulate who your child can interact with and how much private information can be shared.

- Have them add you as a friend no matter how old they are or uncomfortable it makes them feel. Remember, there is no privacy in social networking and knowing you are a member of their site can help them think more carefully about what they post. It is important to review online behavior. Praise great posts as well as guide them about inappropriate posts.
- Make sure they get permission from you to post any pictures. By doing this, parents can review the impulsive post that may be inappropriate before it is too late. After taking this approach for a while your children will better understand the limits you expect when posting pictures.

Many schools offer free parent classes with a presenter who talks about the social media safeguards. These are great sources of information. It is important to realize that there are new sites coming out every few months and parents need to stay up to date.

Television

Parent: Dr. Ron, I wanted to tell you about a funny thing my four-year-old son does. He really loves a certain movie and watches it almost every day, but he hates the scene with the puffer fish. He will get visibly nervous when it is about to come out. As a result, he has learned how to use the remote control and he fast-forwards that part every time. It has become a bit of a joke that he likes the remote

> more than some of his toys. Now that he knows how to use
> it, he keeps the remote with him during the whole movie.
> What do you think that is all about?

The American Academy of Child and Adolescent Psychiatry reported in 2011 that children watch an average of four hours of television per day. That is twenty-eight hours per week and almost fifteen hundred hours per year. To put this in perspective, children spend almost twice as much time watching TV than they spend being instructed by a teacher per year in the United States (that average is 782 hours).[5] At that rate, by the time the average person reaches forty years of age, he or she will have spent more than six years watching TV. Children are also spending a significant amount of their time playing video games. A study showed children eight to eighteen years old spend an average of seven hours and thirty-eight minutes using entertainment media in a typical day. That is more than fifty-three hours per week.[6] This severely limits the amount of time left to develop decision-making and judgment skills.

Television plays a major role in our lives. With today's on-demand cable and DVR technology, we can watch just about whatever we want whenever we want to, and we can skip the parts of the show our children don't like. Not so long ago, we were required to set a VCR to record a show. Not long before that, we needed to actually be there when a show aired to watch it. If a great show was going to air Thursday night at 8:00 p.m., it actually took some real planning to make sure everyone was home, ready, and prepared for the episode. There was no rewind or pause of live television. This may seem a bit dramatic, but it exemplifies the fact that time management, planning, and prioritizing were so much a part of everyday living. In other words, the lack of advanced technology created the opportunity to make mistakes, feel disappointed, and learn from the mistake. Instant 24/7 access takes away opportunities to practice these skills.

Today's parents and children learn the value of instant gratification with television very early. It is not uncommon for infants and toddlers to regularly watch television and videos designed to grab their attention. In fact, some programming is designed just for children under one year old such as the Baby Einstein video collection, and others like it, which claim that there are benefits to having infants watch and listen to the program. The advertising is so powerful that parents are actually made to feel guilty if they don't expose their children to the programs. Infants and young children learn very quickly that parents have the power to start, stop, rewind, pause, and restart television and videos whenever they like, instantly, and their parents will do so when they react in a particular way. That's a lot of power for an infant or young child, and they grow up expecting lots of things to work that way.

Again, these are not conveniences that should be given up. But it is another example of technological advances depriving our children of valuable every day learning experiences. The goal is to utilize the conveniences and benefits of technology, and be aware to provide other learning experiences for your children so they learn patience and problem solving.

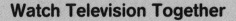

Watch Television Together

Television is a lot like the other technologies discussed in this chapter. In moderation, it is probably just fine, but when it becomes a way to escape responsibility or social opportunities, it can be a hindrance to normal personal and social development. We offer the following tips:

- No televisions in the kids' rooms. It only encourages isolation and separation from the family. When the television is in a common area, you can be sure that the shows being watched are more appropriate.
- Set up family rules for the times and amount of television that can be watched.
- Schedule family television events. They can consist of watching a movie, a show, or a special event (football game, awards show, Discovery series) together. The key is that the family participates as a whole. This can be great family time but it requires planning and organization.
- A lot of really good educational TV programming is available. Nudge your children toward shows about nature, history, or adventure. Shows today are often so visually stimulating; children won't even realize it's good for them. *Myth Busters* is a favorite in our family.

Ask your children what they watched and learned. Mealtime is a wonderful opportunity for talking and letting kids lead the discussion. "I saw you watching a show about volcanoes. I don't really understand them.

How do they work?" Or, "I wonder how close the nearest volcano is. Did you see anything about that?" This encourages your kids to "think" about what they are watching. You can also look for ways to relate these family activities to what they are learning in school.

Technology isn't the problem. However, when the use of these electronics enables a child to miss opportunities to grow or develop skills, we take note. For all the wonders of technologies, in the hands of an impulsive or anxious child, there are some very real fears. If you can't sit through a commercial, how do you sit through school? If the majority of your discussions occur online, what happens when you have to do an in-person interview to get a job? Finally, what happens to the teen who doesn't practice problem solving as a child when he goes off to college and has to make a lot of decisions on his own?

It's important to remember that we don't often consider the long-term impact of our short-term goals. You might use electronics to get a child to stop crying while you are on the phone or to remind her to come home for dinner on time. The use of technology in each of these situations is convenient and makes sense. When it becomes the standard or expectation is when it leads to problems with a dependency on technology.

Putting It All Together

The Issue
Technology makes it really easy to do a lot of things and this is great. As a result, this generation of children knows nothing other than an instant gratification world.

The Trap
We find ourselves in a time where technology is the solution to a lot of problems. Answers are obtained at lightning speed, directions are at our fingertips, and there is no limit to the amount of information, data, and media available to us. The trap occurs when children fail to develop the ability to think for themselves and solve their own problems because they believe that they don't need to. Why think about the earth's circumference when you can search the Internet for the answer in seconds.

The Alternative
Embrace technology as a powerful tool to help your children achieve their dreams. Teach them how to use it positively and it can be a great part of their development.

- From the very beginning, be alert for situations where children appear to be dependent on technology. Maybe they cry until you play the video they want, or they refuse to fall asleep unless they have some electronic device soothing them. When you see this happening, change up the routine and let them learn how to wait or soothe themselves. This goes for older kids too. Pay attention to whether they are glued to a screen during any free time.

- Have your children earn new electronic devices such as video games or phones. The sense of accomplishment is very powerful and reinforcing.
- Know what they are doing online and tell them that you are paying attention to it.
- Participate in social networking with them.
- Have them teach you about new technology or things that they are doing online. It will show you are interested and keep communication open.

Set clear rules and boundaries for use of electronics from the very beginning. Your rules might be no video games on school nights, or no phones at the table, but whatever the agreed-upon rules are, make sure they are enforced.

CHAPTER 9
Athletics Provides More Than Just Fun

A friend of ours was coaching a little league baseball team for eleven-year-olds. The season is more than twenty-five games long and lasts about four months. This particular team made it to the finals of the tournament at the end of the season and earned beautiful runner-up trophies that the boys were very proud of. A few weeks after the season ended, a parent contacted the coach and asked if he could pick up his son's trophy. It took a few minutes for the coach to remember the child, since he had quit the team after four games because he "hated baseball." The child hadn't attended a practice in three months and missed the last twenty-plus games, but the parent thought that after quitting on his teammates, he should still get a tournament trophy.

—Dr. Ron

There was a time when children begged their parents to let them play an organized sport. Today, it seems as if much of this has changed. Parents routinely sign their children up to play a sport without consulting them or asking their child's opinion. It is not uncommon for kids to be playing on teams throughout the year, whether they want to or not. And many parents "coach shop," which means they try to make sure their child always gets the best coach and plays on teams with his friends. Parents become so invested in making the season a positive experience by purchasing the best gear, being on a winning team, and advocating for their child to play a popular position that the child often misses the lessons learned by simply committing to the sport, setting goals, and learning how to communicate with others. In doing so, parents play right into the traps of the Instant Gratification Generation. In previous chapters, we shared that many parents struggle with rescuing their children from the demands of school, but parental overinvolvement in the realm of athletics can also have an impact. These kinds of parental interferences shelter children from dealing with unpredictable circumstances, which means fewer opportunities to build resiliency and overcome obstacles.

Why Should Children Play Sports?

I was at a youth soccer tournament where a friend of mine was coaching a group of ten-year-olds that had just lost the championship game. The kids all got medals and had huge smiles on their faces. There were lots of hugs from parents and talk about a pizza party to celebrate. I mentioned to the coach that they didn't look like a team that just lost and he said that the kids played the best soccer of their season in the tournament and did much better than they expected. To them it was a huge success to play so well and everyone was really proud of how far the kids made it.

—Dr. Ron

Just as teachers, administrators, and parents emphasized that resilience, hard work, and social skills are strong predictors of success for children and adults, the coaches we interviewed highlighted the same characteristics. They reported "diligence," "hard work," "perseverance," and "the ability to look at the big picture" as important characteristics in a successful athlete.

Kids hear terms like *work ethic, practice, teamwork*, and *dedication* frequently from coaches, so they become familiar with those concepts early on. When this is the case, practicing these "life" skills becomes fun and rewarding. When we add in the health benefits of regular exercise, athletics can become a powerful part of a healthy childhood.

Each time our children get together with other kids, they learn how to make and maintain friends, play together, communicate, and a whole host of skills that will be used in their daily lives. Athletics fills this need perfectly. Play comes naturally to the vast majority of children. On the other hand, playing well with others sometimes takes a little more practice. Early childhood offers a great opportunity for children to practice this skill by having them play an organized activity.

While athletics has so much to offer children in the way of teaching diligence, hard work, and perseverance, it can only do that if parents support those lessons. If a parent criticizes a coach, complains about the child's playing time, or rewards the child with trophies when he doesn't play during the season, it undermines what the coaches try to teach their team. When parents step in to orchestrate their child's experience and are working harder than their child for them to be successful, the child can't fully benefit from participation, because she thinks her parent deserves the credit, not her.

Teamwork

Playing on a team provides many great opportunities for a child to learn skills that can be difficult to teach in other environments. Team sports require you to think about other people while at the same time working together toward a mutual goal. The idea that when you work together you can achieve greater success epitomizes what we call teamwork. The metaphors that we use about working together as a team can also be used in so many other contexts.

Parents can be an integral part of supporting teamwork in athletics by partnering with the coach. Sports teams are wrought with social demands. There is the competition between players, social cliques develop, and appropriate and inappropriate joking occurs. While these same issues occur in other environments, on a sports team a coach is present most of the time. If a parent hears about a social challenge with their child, one option is to jump to conclusions, call the other player's parent, and complain to the coach. This might be tempting because it is an immediate reaction to a problem, but it would not teach the child how to deal with it himself and might lead to even more problems for him. The second option is to meet quietly with the coach and gather more information. Then, based on the information supplied by the coach, encourage the child to talk with the coach and figure out some ways to deal with it. Rather than reinforcing an immediate, less effective solution, this alternative reaction would teach the child to take a more thoughtful approach.

Work Ethic

Work ethic is a strong lesson emphasized in youth sports. Just as teachers have young children read every day in the classroom and ask that they read at home, coaches ask the same thing from kids on their teams. A baseball coach will ask kids to practice throwing and catching a ball and swinging a bat. The children who do these things every day, not just at a scheduled practice, build the skill much faster than the ones who don't practice at home. When children see their reading level get better with practice and then they see their throwing, catching, shooting, or kicking getting better with practice, it sends a powerful message: hard work pays off. Because practice is part of the playing on the team it is something they do without questioning it. Very few kids would ask their coach, "Why do we have to have practice? Why can't we just play the games?" because they know the answer. They don't have to be told; they get to experience their team getting better with practice. Kids need to hear that "hard work pays off" over and over again because that knowledge and experience will help them face daunting challenges head on later in life.

This is an extremely valuable lesson to teach children in this Instant Gratification Generation. There is very little instant gratification in athletics. We'll expand on this later in the chapter.

Communication

Another big part of athletics is communication. The more settings in which kids get to practice communication, the better. Playing a sport opens up many new opportunities. To start with, following instructions from a coach can be a new experience for young children. Parents and teachers are the adults they are used to listening to, but they see them daily and don't really see it as a choice. On the other hand, listening to a coach—a brand-new authority figure—can take some getting used to. Coaches often have very strict rules, usually centered on safety, and they enforce them a little differently than teachers and parents.

Most youth coaches who work with very young children understand that the purpose of participation at five or six years old is to foster a love of exercise and organized sports, but as the kids get older, the pampering disappears.

Coaches have a specific goal: to improve the skills of their players while fostering a love of the game and commitment to the team. They constantly communicate with their players throughout practice and games. They may be more or less strict with their players than any individual parent, but our favorite part of the unique communication between coaches and players is the lack of electronics. It is basic verbal communication paired with nonverbal cues. Coaches don't text, email, or instant message their players during practice. They talk to them and model for them what they expect.

When Should Kids Start Playing Organized Sports?

You might be surprised to learn that about thirty-five million children as young as five years old play organized sports each year.[1] It seems as if kids are starting to play younger and more frequently than we might ever have imagined. Youth sports can be broken into four major phases of entry. For the sake of this chapter, we will call them pee wee, youth, juniors, and high school athletics.

Pee Wee

This level of athletics is usually thought of as starting at about five years old or kindergarten. The huge team sports at this age are soccer and T-ball and softball. At this level, the leagues and coaches will often try to keep friends on the same team because they know the goal is to get kids to try a sport and want to play it again in the future. Most of the games or matches at this level are designed to be fun, and it is rare to find a league that actually keeps score. In fact, the kids on both teams typically go home thinking they won, which is great. The idea here is to learn fundamentals and have fun. It is even common to see coaches help kids from the other team.

The skills learned through playing sports at such a young age have the potential to impact these kids for the rest of their lives, and we are not talking about kicking and throwing balls. When a young child gets to learn that practicing something results in better abilities in that skill, there is the opportunity for them to think it could happen outside of sports too. With kids just beginning to develop their work habits for school, the timing couldn't be better. In a generation of young people who don't always learn the value of hard work, practice, and discipline, starting to play athletics at such a young age can introduce those values.

Youth

This period is probably best thought of as starting with kids about eight years old (third grade) to twelve years old (sixth grade). A couple of things happen at this level that are different from the pee-wee leagues. The most important change is that a lot more sports are open to this age group. The major sports like football, lacrosse, volleyball, hockey, water polo, and basketball begin around this age and they attract huge numbers of kids and a heightened level of competitiveness.

A notable difference in athletics at this level is that coaches put together teams to win. Leagues begin to do away with participation trophies, and teams are comprised through a draft to balance skill level, instead of based on friendships. Practice will be a bit more physical, and the coaches will start to expect more from the children.

This is also a wonderful time for kids to be learning something new about themselves. Athletics at this level begin to require some patience and planning, which are great skills for a generation of kids that are generally impulsive and distractible. If you want to be good in any particular sport, you need to understand it and put yourself in position to be successful. In sports, that means being aware of what is about to happen and plan for it. To do this, one must pay attention to a lot of details, consider others, and be proactive. Because natural opportunities to practice this are rare in this generation, sports offer an alternate chance for similar practice.

Try It First

As children reach the age of youth sports, parents roll out many reasons for not signing up their children to play. One of the most common is that registering to play in a league is a big commitment in terms of time and money for something you don't know if your child will even enjoy. To address this issue, we recommend participating in a sports camp (such as through your local rec center) to learn the rules, basic components, and equipment requirements and costs before signing up to play on a team for the first time. The commitment is much less, and if children like the sport and decide for themselves to play for the first time, then they will have a nice foundation of skills for the first practice, which will increase their confidence.

Juniors

The next phase in the progression of youth athletics occurs when kids are twelve or thirteen years old, which loosely coincides with middle school. Most children interested in trying a sport either will have already started their leagues or will enter a league at this time. Even if it is a sport that doesn't have younger age divisions, many of the kids playing will have been practicing the fundamentals at home or with friends.

In juniors sports, many advanced players will have moved to competitive leagues, and it is understood that recreational leagues are for all levels. Around this age kids move from elementary school to middle school, and being a part of a team is another way to expand a child's social connections. It is also a good time for children to begin to learn how to manage multiple responsibilities such as homework, social time, and commitment to a team.

High School

Being a part of a high school athletic team can be a really rewarding experience. The level of competition is often very high by this point. Some of the sports teams can have kids who may have been playing the sport for as long as ten years before trying out for the high school team. For the kids who haven't been very involved in athletics or never found a sport they were passionate about, there are still opportunities available. Some teams take everyone who goes out for the team regardless of skill level or number of years of experience. For instance, it is not uncommon for the freshman football team to take all the boys who go out for the team. In addition, other sports like track and cross-country and swimming and diving welcome everyone because they can field large teams.

Parents Have a Role to Play Too

Even though it is your child who is actually playing on the team, as a parent you have responsibilities too. We admit that there is a fine line between being helpful to your child and being overwhelming. The following guidelines offer suggestions for parent responsibilities at each level of sports.

Pee Wee

The primary responsibility to is to make sure your child arrives on time to practice and games with all his equipment, a bottle of water, and some food in his stomach. After the game, don't ever be critical of your child's performance. Instead, point out good things and always mention how proud you are of your child. The goal here is to get your child to want to continue playing athletics.

Youth

At this level, children really need to find time to practice the fundamental skills of their particular sport. As a parent, you will probably either need to remind your child to practice with her friends or offer to practice with her if you can. Make it fun and try to get your young athlete to see the relationship between skill building and their play during games. Again, after the games stay positive, but feel free to point out some fundamental things that your child might want to work on before the next game.

Juniors

Your focus here should be on gauging your child's interest in the sport and drive to get better. If your child asks for your help, be prepared to spend significant time and effort helping him or her get better.

High School

The responsibility for the parent here changes significantly. You certainly support your child when she asks for help or assistance, but in the big picture, you have to give up almost all interactions with the coaches unless they ask for some parental support, which is likely to be in the form of fund-raising. Instead, you need to make sure your child is getting enough nutritious food, good sleep, and has time to balance her academic responsibilities with her athletic ones.

Recreational Leagues vs. Competitive Club Teams

I met with a family who wanted some advice about how to balance sports and school. Their son had just entered high school and was playing a sport on one of the school's teams. The parents checked their son's grades online and discovered that he had several Cs and Ds. They were rightfully conflicted about their commitment to their son's education and the commitment he made to the team. One of the obvious choices was to pull him from the team. I asked the parents if they had made the coach aware of their son's situation and what his thoughts were, and they

had not. The family met with the coach the very next day,
and the son told his coach how bad his grades had gotten.
When they asked for the coach's thoughts, he suggested
that instead of attending practice with the rest of the team,
the boy should do extra conditioning before school and
meet with tutors after school until he had all Cs or better.
The coach didn't let him practice with the team until his
grades improved, but he didn't kick him off the team either.
The parents avoided having to pull their son from the team
and angering his teammates and coaches while trying to
keep his poor grades secret. I hear that he never worked
harder at school or his sport.

—Dr. Ron

When making the choice to play competitive or recreational sports, the child's home and school responsibilities need to be part of the equation. In order to teach children and teens how to balance multiple responsibilities, everything must be considered, not just their preferred activities. Just because a child is an excellent athlete doesn't mean he should take on the commitment of an advanced league, especially if his schedule doesn't allow for it.

Parents also need to do some self-evaluation and determine whether the drive to play athletics is coming from their child or whether it stems from the parents' interest in the sport or desire for their child to be on an advanced team. It is not uncommon for parents to be highly invested in having their children play the same sports they played as a youth. We sometimes encounter parents who, from a very early age, have made their child play the same sport that they excelled at, almost as a continuation of the parents' success in their own childhood. This leaves the child with little choice but to follow his parent's wishes or risk disappointing his mom or dad. We encourage parents to let their children find the sports that suit the child's interests and passions.

You *Can* Have Too Much of a Good Thing

Participation in athletics can be beneficial to children for many reasons, but there is a limit to how much is enough. The following are signs that the benefits of athletics might not be worth the consequences.

- If you find yourself feeling more invested in the sport than your child, take a careful look at what's motivating your child to play. Is she truly interested in and passionate about the sport, or is it possible she is feeling pressured by you to keep playing?
- If your child does not have enough time or energy to study or complete homework assignments, or the quality of his schoolwork suffers because of fatigue, consider cutting back the amount of practice time.
- If your child suffers from multiple sports-related injuries, speak with her doctor or coach. It might be a good idea to take a season off to help heal her body.

Athletics should be a privilege, so if your child can't follow the family rules, consider linking participation with expectations at home. For example, say, "You can only participate in the travel soccer league this fall if you regularly assist us with chores."

Let the Coaches Do the Coaching

In discussing the role parents take in their child's high school athletics, a nationally known and highly respected high school wrestling coach told us that he asks the parents to support the coaches completely. He tells parents, "I'm going to help you raise your son for the next four years because you're going to need me." His experience is that a great coach can teach your children things in ways parents can't, which include things like perseverance, dedication, commitment, and discipline. He said that when parents play a strong role in supporting the child's efforts by making sure he gets nutritious food to eat, plenty of sleep, and time for schoolwork, the coach and parents can work as a team in meeting these goals together. He can then support the parents in teaching their children to respect the rules of the home, being responsible, and being a positive family member.

It is easy to see that there are a number of significant advantages to having your child play youth sports. There is no doubt that athletics has the potential to play a big role in the lives of children. One of the biggest reasons is the role of the coach. Coaches expect a lot of things from their athletes and they communicate with them in ways not often found in the classroom or at home. In addition, their position as a leader and authority figure that the players respect, offers a unique opportunity to be heard. A high school coach said it best: "We have a better platform as a coach because they want to please and they want to make the team." Good coaches make an impact on the development of children and great coaches help raise them. Coaching is a lot more than telling kids what position they play or how to kick a ball farther. It is a complex relationship that grows in intensity and breadth the older the child gets. It involves being a role model, a motivator, a confidant, and an inspirational leader. So as a parent, we need to let them do their job.

Many parents of athletes become very invested in their child's sport and become "sideline coaches," at times overruling things the coaches says or does. In doing so, the child's participation becomes family participation, but that is unfair to the child. Not only is it important for children to follow the guidance of their coach, but if a parent is overinvested, it takes away from the child's accomplishments. If the child does well, she doesn't feel like she earned the achievement on her own. In the same way, if there is a challenge and the overinvested parent gets involved, it takes away the opportunity for the child to solve the problem on her own. Both instances take away the child's opportunity to grow and gain confidence. In addition, when parents can't let go, especially in high school, they are sending the message to their children that they don't trust them to accomplish their goals own their own. It can make them feel like their parent sees them as incapable or not good enough.

Involve the Coaches in More Than Coaching

Parents sometimes ask our opinion about how to resolve an issue involving athletics. Sometimes a child's grades or attitude around the house slip if he is spending a lot of time on a sport. Other times there may be a disagreement between a child and a parent about what it means to make a commitment to be a part of a sports team.

Our first response is almost always, "Have you

asked the coach what she (or he) thinks?" We believe that coaches are a great resource for parents.

A powerful experience is to request a family meeting with the coach and have your child present the issues at hand. If your child is mature enough, have him make the first contact with the coach. It is often difficult for a child to tell his coach about poor grades, being disrespectful at home, or a lack of commitment, but it is a great opportunity for him to learn how to talk about difficult issues with nonfamily members. The overwhelming majority of coaches value the behavior and attitude of their athletes when away from the playing field or court. You are likely to find them very supportive of your concerns and eager to offer valuable opinions about how to proceed.

The Ultimate Benefit of Athletics

Throughout this book, we have spent a lot of time discussing the skills and abilities that are so important for children and teens to practice in the formative years. Now let's look at how these skills and abilities are specifically emphasized in athletics.

Getting Better Takes Time and Work

With the Instant Gratification Generation, children and teens come to expect everything quickly. Perseverance and working toward a goal can be difficult qualities to instill in this generation. With athletics, there is no way around it.

To learn a sport, a child needs to experience hours of practice and coaching to get better. It doesn't matter how coordinated or fast she might be; she needs to teach her muscles to move the way she wants them to for a particular sport. That comes with a lot of practice. Children are dependent on themselves to put in the work. There are no shortcuts.

There are children who are athletically gifted and can pick up almost any sport and play well. But you will notice that even these kids work hard to get better. In fact, it is so reinforcing for them to be a strong player on the team, you will find these kids love to practice.

Direct Interpersonal Communication (without Electronics!)

As we've seen in previous chapters, much of the communication between today's children and teens is through electronic devices, particularly text messaging. With sports, they are required to actually talk to each other through direct communication. They need to be aware of their nonverbal cues, such as tone of voice and body language so they don't come across as a bad sport when giving feedback, and they need to be able to clearly communicate to each other during a game to set up and execute plays. Athletes are also required to communicate with their coach respectfully. Additionally, the opportunity to learn how to support their peers when they make a mistake, and feel comfortable with doing so, is invaluable.

Low-Cost Risk Taking

Children and teens of this generation become accustomed to being rescued any time they encounter a challenge. In this way, they are reluctant to take risks, and this is true with athletics too. When they begin playing sports at a young age, it offers them a wonderful opportunity to try something new with very low risk. They can try several different sports and see which one they like.

In addition, if children do not do well when they first try something, they often tend to want to quit. Committing to a sports team offers an opportunity for them to stick with something even if they change their mind. No one will come in and rescue them to ease their discomfort. They will actually have to stick it out. Aside from the frustration you hear from your child, the negative consequences for sticking it out are very limited and the positive consequences are abundant.

For many children, after the one or two days that they are frustrated and want to quit a sport, things typically get better. When they end up enjoying the sport, they may learn that their first impulse isn't always the best. It also teaches them that they can survive discomfort and that their parents won't allow them to quit something just because it gets difficult.

Balance Multiple Responsibilities

Playing sports offers children and teens the opportunity to practice balancing multiple responsibilities. As noted, school and family responsibilities need to come first. Then they can add things of their choosing. Playing sports is a great motivator for them to manage their school and family responsibilities well, because it allows them the reward of participating in other activities that they really enjoy.

Anytime you can set your children up to build skills of organization, planning, and decision making, it is a great thing. Playing sports offers this opportunity.

What If Your Child Isn't Interested in Sports?

This chapter focused on the role that athletics can play in a child's life and the benefits of participating in organized sports. However, many activities can provide these same experiences. If your child is not interested in sports, you can apply these same tips and recommendations to the activity of their choice.

- Playing an instrument requires practice and perseverance to get better. It also offers the opportunity to receive coaching from another adult. Playing in an orchestra, band, or ensemble offers the same sense of teamwork and commitment that playing on a sports teams does.
- Participating in Scouts or a similar organized group can also offer the same opportunities. Scouts have to work to earn badges, participate in community service activities, and communicate with others (peers, adults, and community members).
- Theater is very similar to playing on a sports team. It has a significant time commitment, and your child will need to learn to manage personal responsibilities with rehearsals. In addition, adult coaches teach and model the craft for the cast. And again, practice is essential to getting better and earning the roles your child may want.

Almost all the teachers, parents, and coaches that we talked with said that they see irreplaceable benefits from having children participate in organized activities—sports being one. It offers children a constructive alternative to spending hours on electronic devices, helps increase confidence in their skills, introduces a balance to their self-identity, and keeps them comfortable interacting with others in multiple environments, not to mention the positive influence of having other adult mentors in their life. There aren't many opportunities that offer these same gifts for children and adolescents.

Putting It All Together

The Issue
We want our children to be happy, successful, and popular. In athletics, that often manifests as being the star player on the winning team with the best coach and the coolest uniforms. It means winning the biggest trophies and having all your friends on the team. Parents enjoy sharing with other people the athletic accomplishments of their children.

The Trap
It is so easy for parents to get caught up in making athletics the perfect experience for their children, especially if sports were a large part of their own childhood. You may want to find out which coach has won the most and maneuver your child to be on that team. You also may feel the need to buy the best and most expensive gear, even if it doesn't help him hit a ball better or run faster.

The Alternative

When your child is young, the leagues support many of the issues discussed earlier. They put friends together on teams, make the kids feel like they always win, and often give participation trophies. If this is important to you and your child, then make sure you start your child in athletics during the pee wee stage. There are a lot of great opportunities for kids who are five or six years old.

As children get older, fewer of these comforts will be available. It is important to resist the temptation to jump in and rescue them. If they get selected on a team without their friends, talk to them about the opportunity to make new friends and support their new friendships. If they don't think the coach is playing them in the right position, it is a great opportunity to have them approach the coach to discuss it. Often the coach will listen and offer suggestions about how they might achieve their goal, many times through hard work and practice. Also, remember that if your child's team isn't winning a lot, it is OK. Kids on those teams often work harder and appreciate winning even more than the teams that win because of having gifted athletes, instead of hard work.

Finally, seek out opportunities to use the coach as a mentor and role model. Expect your child to treat the coach with respect and utilize the coach's role to support you in setting expectations for your child. Equally important, do not criticize the coach in front of your children because it diminishes the value of the coach as a leader for all the coaches to follow.

Chapter 10

Why Drugs and Alcohol Are So Appealing

Teenager: Dr. Darlene, I have been looking online and it says that smoking pot is just fine. I can show you one hundred articles that say there is no problem with it. I am sure that it is true.

Teens have always presented themselves as invincible and confident in their knowledge of how the world works. Today's Instant Gratification Generation is no exception. If a teen has an interest in substance use, she will find online resources that prove drugs, alcohol, or both are safe, and she will believe wholeheartedly that the information is evidence that her parents and teachers are all wrong. However, sources are often faulty, along with the teenager's rationale.

Recent research presented by CNN Health suggests that when it comes to drugs and alcohol, teens are actually more vulnerable to negative effects on the brain than adults.[1] Young people have more receptors in their brains with which drugs and alcohol can bind, creating more opportunity for brain damage and inhibiting personal development. Since so much is going on in the developing brain, drugs have a greater potential to change the trajectory of brain development for the worse. While many teenagers think that marijuana use is safe, verified research using functional magnetic resonance imaging (fMRI) indicates that the frontal and the prefrontal areas of the brain are negatively affected by cannabis use.[2] Reflecting back on findings discussed in chapter 5, you will remember that the frontal lobe of the brain is continuing to develop into early adulthood. Further, the frontal lobe is the part of the brain that guides executive functioning (e.g., planning, organizing, decision making, problem solving). The teen years are crucial to strengthening these abilities, not damaging them.

Why This Generation Is So Susceptible to Substance Use and Abuse

Drugs and alcohol may not be a defining characteristic of the Instant Gratification Generation, but illicit substances certainly play a role in their lives. This is, after all, a group of young people that has difficulty with delayed gratification, which means these teens can't tolerate waiting for things. They often look for the fastest solution to problems, not the best, and many teens truly believe that nothing bad will happen to them if they use substances, despite mounds of evidence to the contrary. Their desire for the quick answer leads them to act without thinking things through, or to disregard their own conscience if they do think about what they are about to do.

The Failure to Think Things Through

We have raised a generation of children who need and come to expect quick solutions to problems, as we demonstrate throughout this book. This means that they aren't required to think things through, which encourages them to act impulsively.

Because children and teens are so accustomed to getting things quickly, kids in this generation are less likely to take the time to consider all the outcomes of their decisions. This generation is the most educated about the dangers of drug use and the drugs today are more dangerous than ever, but none of that has kept them from using.[3] Their desire to get what they want outweighs the requirement for them to wait and be thoughtful before they act. They pay attention to what is in front of them in the moment. If it is what they want, they act on it. Teens are generally impulsive anyway, but add the reinforcement of instant gratification in this generation and they are even more vulnerable to follow the impulse to use drugs to fit in, relieve boredom, rebel, and so on.

> *A seventeen-year-old boy was in my office upset at his parents because he was grounded for getting caught drinking over the weekend. He proceeded to tell me that he should not get in so much trouble for having only one beer. This was all his parents knew of the night, so, of course, that is what their arguments were about. He then told me he drank five beers that night and then rode in the car with the friend who was the "most sober" to another party. He boasted that his friends are careful to choose one person who only drinks a little so they have a ride. He did not even consider the consequences of what could have happened. He was very shortsighted in several ways. First, he was truly upset with his parents for the consequence they gave him for drinking "only one beer," even though he did much more that night. Second, he was so focused on*

having fun that he did not even consider the potentially deadly outcome of drinking and driving.

—Dr. Darlene

Would it surprise you to know that the boy in the vignette is an A student who spends a lot of time doing community service? He is a bright kid who generally thinks of others. So, why did he act so irresponsibly? In many ways, society has reinforced the idea of thinking quickly. Starting in school, the first child to raise her hand gets to answer the teacher's question, the first kid to the four-square court gets to make the rules even if they are silly rules and poorly thought out. Parents need to be aware of this phenomenon and let their children know that in some situations taking their time and thinking about options is a good idea. Alternately, when they see the signs and symptoms of reckless drug or alcohol use, they need to react quickly and set limits. We discuss how parents can identify signs and set limits throughout this chapter.

In our work with children and teens, we often use the idea of the STOPP sign. This is an easy way to help children organize their thoughts before they make an important decision. STOPP stands for **S**top, **T**hink, **O**bserve, **P**lan, **P**roceed. The idea is to consider the risks and the benefits of a decision before making it. Simply getting them to stop and think is a great first step. Another great thing about the STOPP sign is that it is easy for parents to use and reinforce at home.

Parents Need to Be Very Aware

One thing we have learned, in all our years working with teenagers, is that parents are not always good judges of which friends are the responsible ones. Time and time again parents will tell us which of their child's friends they trust and then their teen will come in and laugh, because she says the friend her parents thinks is responsible in fact drinks or smokes more than anyone else. It is important to remember that the friendliest and most socially competent child isn't always the one following the rules. We wish we could tell you how to know who is trustworthy and who is not, but there are no tried-and-true ways. The best thing is to be around your child and her friends in social situations as much as possible, observing how they interact with each other. Providing rides or opening your house for them to hang out is a great way to do that.

Parents should also be aware of the "street names" that kids use when talking about drugs. Most of us are familiar with the mainstream drug references, like "pot" for marijuana, but there are a lot of new drugs, many of them synthetic, that kids can actually find in liquor stores and head shops. Children often discuss substances like K2, Spice, salvia, bath salts, molly, and a host of others right in front of adults, because the adults simply don't know what they are talking about. An easy way for parents to keep up is to visit websites, such as www.drugfree.org, where they can learn just about anything about drugs.[4]

You should continually stay informed about who your child's friends are and what is going on in the community. Make an effort to check in with your children and keep an open mind regarding what you hear. Don't take what they say for granted. It is a powerful message to them when they know you are interested in what is going on in their lives, whether or not they ultimately share anything with you.

Things Need to Be Fun All the Time

I hear far too frequently about how kids make the trip to the local grocery store or pharmacy when they are bored to grab a packet of cold medicine. They don't pay for it; they simply open it in the store, split up the pills, and hope they get a buzz. Cold medicine tends to dehydrate you and the kids say that if you take enough you get a hallucinogenic feeling for a short time. Of the kids who have told me this story, several of them have ended up in the emergency room because they were bored and wanted some excitement but overdosed by accident instead.

—Dr. Ron

Children and teens in this generation are bombarded with stimulating information from early on. They become accustomed to needing that constant excitement. As illustrated in the foregoing example, very often we hear stories of the children and teens we work with getting in trouble with drugs and alcohol because they were bored and the substances were available.

Because children and teens tend to act impulsively on opportunity, they may seek out items from around the house, like bottles from unlocked alcohol cabinets, prescription drugs from their parent's medicine cabinet, and over-the-counter medicines that can get them high if taken the "wrong" way. We recommend that every parent be aware of what alcohol and prescription drugs are in the house and periodically take an informal inventory. If the medicine cabinet contains a pill bottle with five Vicodin left over from a minor surgery, check every now and again to make sure the pills are all there. Another option is to remove prescription drugs from the medicine cabinet altogether and store them where your teen (or their friends) can't access them.

Self-Medicating

A family brought their fifteen-year-old son to see me because they were concerned he had a drinking problem. They discovered that he had been drinking alcohol at home and at school several times per week. They were looking for a referral for a teen alcohol program and guidance about what they should do as a family. It didn't take long for me to conclude that the underlying issue was peer related and that he drank as a way of escaping the negative thoughts he had about himself and his deteriorating relationship with his friends. He chose alcohol as self-medication, his preferred way to handle his emotions, because he had never had to solve a problem like this before on his own. Once he stopped self-medicating, and with some help, he was able to come up with some effective ways to manage his stress and friendships in a healthier way. He now has a plan for what to do when he has negative thoughts about his friends that may or may not be justified.

—Dr. Ron

It is not uncommon for people to use an illicit substance to help them cope with stress. People who are feeling withdrawn might look for something to give them a little boost of energy, and those with social phobias have been known to drink alcohol or take other depressants as a way of dealing with their nerves around others. We probably all know someone who takes a pill before she flies on a plane or speaks in front of a crowd to help with anxiety.

The Instant Gratification Generation takes it one step further. Many children and adolescents have developed an amazingly low threshold for dealing with any kind of anxiety, low self-esteem, or frustration. This puts them at high risk to turn to substances to help them "forget" their problems, because they do not want to or know how to deal with them. First, the pressure for this generation to perform at high levels is significant. Second, as we have highlighted in previous chapters, they don't have the practice to know how to deal with problems and feel confident they can solve them. So when they are presented an opportunity to forget about those problems for a while and their attitude is "I don't care," it is very easy to turn to substances as an escape.

The concept of self-medicating is also appealing to the Instant Gratification Generation because it is easy. They have a problem, they don't have confidence they can deal with it, and there is a quick way to avoid the problem and feel better. Yet kids only think about what the drug can do *for* them, not what it is doing *to* them. What might feel great one night may actually impact the rest of their lives, and in a way that is slow enough that they fail to see the link. If you feel fine the next day, drugs or alcohol must be OK to use again and again. The false sense of security gained by being narrow-minded and impulsive gives these kids the belief that they will be fine no matter what they do. Nothing can be further from the truth; they just haven't learned it yet.

It Won't Happen To Me

In a 2012 study, nearly 25 percent of teens surveyed reported that, within the previous month, they had ridden in a car with someone who had been drinking alcohol, and almost 10 percent admitted to driving after drinking in the same month.[5] One third of the young drivers killed in car crashes had alcohol in their system, but teens insist that they will never be a statistic.[6] Nearly 150,000 teens experience an accidental drug overdose each year, and it is likely that few of them thought it would happen to them.[7]

We have demonstrated how youth today are highly impulsive and look for easy solutions to their problems. There is another quality they possess that plays a major role in their decisions about using illegal substances: denial. A person in denial is someone who refuses to pay attention to the facts. Schools are saturated with negative messages about the horrors of teen drug use. High schools display demolished cars involved in drunk driving accidents, and children as early as kindergarten take antidrug pledges. Parents, teachers, religious leaders, and law enforcement officials talk about the dangerous consequences of drug or alcohol abuse all the time, and yet, teenagers honestly believe that none of what they learn will happen to them.

Rationalization

During a session with a high school junior enrolled at a competitive private school, I learned that he had been buying Adderall during finals week. Adderall is a medication prescribed by psychiatrists to help treat ADHD/ADD because it helps improve concentration. It is a substance commonly sold illegally on college campuses during finals to help students study for exams. And in the past several years, we have heard this same thing from high school kids too. This particular student needed certain grades to qualify for his top college choices and was willing to do anything to get the best grades. Buying illegal prescription drugs and taking them without a doctor's guidance is a huge risk to take to reduce his anxiety about doing well on exams.

—Dr. Ron

"It's organic." "It's all natural." "What's the difference if I buy it at school or get it prescribed from a doctor? It's the same drug." These are just a few of the things we hear from children and teens who use illegal substances. Kids today offer a lot of excuses as to why it is OK for them to ingest whatever they want, and they put a lot of effort into finding reasons that their behavior should be acceptable to parents and concerned adults. In fact, they can spend a lot of time on the Internet searching for evidence to support their beliefs.

Kids want what they want, and they will find all sorts of reasons to confirm their beliefs. One form of rationalization is called "confirmatory bias." This means the person is only looking for evidence that supports his or her theory. Therefore, when kids are looking for reasons their impulsive and dangerous behavior should be acceptable, they focus on information that supports their belief and ignore all the evidence that says otherwise. It is true that the Internet is full of articles that support drug use, but a lot of research also highlights the dangers. They just don't pay attention to those contrary articles. In many ways, they have been trained to rely on the first piece of information that supports their ideas. Internet search engines are organized to put the best match at the top of the list, and we know that is the way they search for information. What do you expect to find at the top of the list when you search for "marijuana is not dangerous"?

Help Teens Navigate the Evidence

When talking with teens about substance use, they are going to assume that your views are biased because you are old or trying to trick them. They often feel they know better and have more up-to-date information. Sharing your views without evidence to back them up is likely to elicit doubt. It can be really helpful to find some data to show how substances impact them in a physical sense. That way you are sharing not just your opinion but facts. For example, Elizabeth Lander's article, "Teen Brain More Prone to Drug, Alcohol Damage," shows how substance use impacts the adolescent brain.[8]

When they show you their evidence that using substances is OK, go through it with them and educate them about what they are reading. It might help to have prepared for this exercise by spending some time reading up on the balanced research being done by reputable universities and research laboratories.

Signs of Drug and Alcohol Use

A family came in to see me for some parenting advice. They found some marijuana in their son's dresser drawer and weren't sure how to handle it. They were relieved to hear that their son was actually only holding it for a friend who couldn't bring it home that day after school. A few weeks later, a package was delivered to the home that contained several glass tubes similar to ones used in a chemistry lab, but also just like the ones used to smoke drugs. Since it worked the first time, the boy said they were "for a friend." He stated that he knew nothing about the package and that one of his friends must have ordered it and had it delivered to his house so he wouldn't get caught by his own parents. I pointed out to the family that as much as they wanted to believe their son's stories, they needed to pay attention to the obvious signs of drug use, and we developed a plan to address it.

—Dr. Ron

In other parts of this book, we encouraged letting children make mistakes in the hope that they will learn important lessons about solving problems. Use or abuse of illicit drugs and alcohol is *not* one of those situations. With drug use, the risk of mental, physical, or emotional problems following each incident warrants careful monitoring and action when needed.

Parents need to be aware of what to look for when determining if their child is using drugs or alcohol. It is too important to his health and safety to overlook or ignore warning signs. Being familiar with the signs of drug and alcohol use is a great place to start. These signs can essentially be broken down into two broad categories: changes in behavior and changes in appearance.

Changes in Behavior

- **Subtle Signs:** In most cases, an abrupt change to a child's behavior is generally rare, so you need to pay attention to gradual changes in behavior. Some of the most common early behavioral signs of drug and alcohol use include being unusually tired, excessively angry, and very secretive. Drug and alcohol use is associated with a decrease in motivation and being withdrawn from their usual friends and activities.

- **Overt Signs:** A lack of balance or coordination is a common sign during or directly after substance use. Consider violations of curfew, sneaking out, and money problems to be serious issues that can be associated with using, selling, or acquiring substances. You may see an increase in secretive communications with new friends and a vigilant attempt to keep emails, phone calls, and texts private by immediately deleting them. An increase in aggression including volatile arguments and fighting may occur as well.

Changes in Appearance

- **Subtle Signs:** None of these are surefire indicators of drug use, but they are still important markers to examine. Look for changes in hygiene, poor personal grooming, and a messy appearance. Kids who use drugs and alcohol start to look physically different too. Significant and rapid weight loss or weight gain can be directly related to certain classes of substances.
- **Overt Signs:** When someone is using or has recently used drugs and alcohol, you may see red or flushed cheeks and difficulty focusing his eyes on something specific. Another serious sign to consider may be burns on his lips or fingers, bruising, signs he has been in fights, and signs that he may not be in good health.

Talk about It

If you have witnessed signs that lead you to believe that your child is drinking or using drugs, it is important to come right out and ask her about it. Research indicates that children develop better self-control and have more negative perceptions about substance use behaviors when parents and children can talk openly about drugs and alcohol. Ignoring the signs and hoping that they go away on their own is simply too risky.

My Kids Wouldn't Do That

In our counseling practices, we see a lot of kids who are responsible, doing well in school, respectful to adults, and pretty open with their parents. But even those kids are exposed to drug and alcohol use and are not immune to the temptations of all other teenagers. It is really important that parents remain aware of the risks and signs even if they don't feel that their children are vulnerable to making the choice to drink or do drugs.

Help Your Child Practice Making Excuses

At some point, most children are faced with the opportunity to say yes or no when offered alcohol or drugs. It would be great if every child were able to look her friends in the eye and say that she didn't want to use substances or drink alcohol, but for many children and teens, this is not easy. If your child doesn't have the ability to simply say no, having an excuse is a great alternative. A helpful gift to give your children is an excuse that is accepted by their friends. The following are some of the good ones:

- "My parents drug test me every week, and if I test positive, I have to enter a drug rehab program."
- "My parents bought one of those Breathalyzers, and they test me when I get home at night. If I test positive, I lose my license."
- "I have tried that, but it's not my thing."

Whether students are attracted to drugs and alcohol because they want to be socially accepted, to avoid the stress they are feeling, to enhance their performance, or simply to have fun, they are adamantly finding reasons to justify that their choices are safe. They want a quick answer and they are impulsively acting on the easiest solution that feels good in the moment, which is the core risk for the Instant Gratification Generation.

Putting It All Together

The Issue
It is scary to think about the possibility that your child may be exposed to drugs or alcohol—or even use them. If you have these concerns, it requires a lot of time, monitoring, and conflict with your child. It is a huge commitment to do what it takes to monitor it closely. Many parents are too anxious about what they will find or how to deal with it to address the issue with their children directly.

The Trap
Children and teens aren't the only ones who believe "it will never happen to them." Parents also are reluctant to consider their children making the choice to use alcohol or do drugs, particularly if they are generally considerate and do well in school. Parents tend to focus more on the progress toward college than keeping up to date on the latest fads in drug use and whether their children are showing signs of use. Don't let yourself fall into the trap of denial.

The Alternative
Throughout this book, we encourage parents to allow their children and teens to make mistakes and learn lessons and skills from the consequences that follow. When drug and alcohol use are involved, this is not the case. There are serious risks with substance use, and parents need to be actively involved in monitoring and guiding their children.

When parents and children can have healthy conversations about drug and alcohol use, it actually reduces the likelihood of problems developing down the road. Having clear understandings about the illegal use of substances and the consequences of using is another important conversation to have. Always let your children know that you love them enough to take appropriate steps to keep them healthy. Along these lines, parents need to be aware of the signs and symptoms of drug and alcohol use and not ignore them if they are present. If parents suspect their child is using drugs or alcohol in a manner that concerns them, they must act. Too much is on the line to sit back and hope that things will turn out for the best.

Chapter 11

Will Your Child Be Ready to Launch?

I received a frantic call from a couple wanting consultation about their nineteen-year-old daughter who failed to finish her first semester at an elite university. The mother shared that "they" worked very hard for her to earn the grades and SAT scores to be accepted into this school and she was confused about what happened. She went on to say that she made sure her daughter had the best tutoring, reputable SAT prep, and she edited all her daughter's high school papers to make sure that she was doing high-caliber work. The family was thrilled when her daughter was accepted into the college of her choice and wanted to know what went wrong.

—Dr. Darlene

Don't Stop Teaching

Chances are, you recognized yourselves—and your children—in the previous chapters of this book. Mistakes were made on both sides, and opportunities to let your child practice independent problem-solving and critical-thinking skills may have been missed. It's all part of raising a child in the Instant Gratification Generation, and you are probably wondering what to do now that your child is a teenager. Don't give up. It will be difficult to undo the patterns your child has developed, but it is possible. If he or she is in the last two years of high school (or was not successful at "flying solo" when leaving home the first time), there are several things to do to teach the skills of conscientious planning, decision making, and goal-oriented actions.

Driving

Driving offers the perfect opportunity to teach the skills required for an adult to lead a conscientious and independent life. Think about all the things that are required to have the privilege of driving. A person must do the following things:

- The person must take the initiative to sign up and complete a driver's education course.
- The person must prepare, schedule, take, and pass the driving test.
- The person must organize time to do this around other responsibilities (e.g., school, sports, music, chores).
- The person must be conscientious of others on the road.
- The person must pay attention to multiple things going on at once.
- The person must utilize planning and problem solving with driving directions and time management.
- The person must practice delayed gratification. If he hears his cell phone chirp while driving, he can't look at or answer it.

- The person must earn money for gas, insurance, and vehicle maintenance.
- The person must set limits with peers around being the "driver" all the time or letting others ride in the car before they are legally able.

Parents tend to get very excited (as well as worried) about their children driving. They remember when they were fifteen or sixteen and got their learner's permit. Then on their sixteenth birthday, or soon thereafter, they were at the Department of Motor Vehicles to get their license. This was easier a generation or two ago when driver's education was taught at school and the coursework required was planned into a teenager's schedule. Now many teenagers have to take a driver's education course on their own time through a private company. Guess what? This requires planning and organization, as well as initiative on the part of the teenager to meet the goal.

An important concept for parents to remember is that if a teenager does not have the skills to organize the information needed to sign up for driver's education and complete and pass the class on his or her own, then he or she doesn't have the level of responsibility needed to be driving a car.

Don't Push Them to Get a License

If teenagers are not showing the responsibility to register for and take the driver's education courses themselves, they should not be pushed, bribed, nagged, or enticed in any other way by their parents. Many times, they are not doing it due to a lack of organization or even laziness, which is even more reason to wait until they show the initiative to do it on their own.

If a teenager is emotionally ready to drive, but too lazy or dependent on others to get a license, it is important for his mom and dad to stop making it too easy. Parents should not support their teens by continuing to drive them around. Instead, if they stop being their child's shuttle service, he will need to get a license to go where he wants to go.

How It Works

1. Rides should only be to and from school if the walk is too far; otherwise, walking should occur several times per week. Typically, a parent is around to give the ride to school, but it is not always convenient to be back for the ride home. If it is not convenient and the walking distance is safe and reasonable, have her walk home.
2. For any social activities, she will need to start finding her own rides. If she doesn't have a ride, she can't go to the activity. Again, at times it may be convenient for the parent to give her a ride and that is OK, but this can't be the norm.
3. Don't go out of your way to change your schedule for unplanned rides to various destinations, such as activities, to purchase things, to see a friend, unless it is to meet one of her responsibilities.

The Response

"I know you want me to drive you there, but I am not available. When you are ready, you can sign up for (or finish) that driver's education course. Then you will be able to earn your own driver's license."

Managing Money

A thirteen-year-old girl got her first cell phone. The phone was intended for emergencies and so she could communicate with her parents. Her parents set up a limited data and usage plan. After the first month, they saw that she went over her minutes and was texting her friends; therefore, they increased her plan to include unlimited texting and more minutes. They talked with their daughter and set strict limits on her data usage. Despite their instructions, she downloaded so many programs that she far surpassed her data usage plan. Her parents succumbed and gave her unlimited data usage. At the end of six months, their twenty-dollars-per-month plan ballooned into a one-hundred-dollar monthly expense.

—Dr. Ron

We can emphatically tell you that in our experience, one of the best predictors of dysfunction is when children and teens have few or no limits when it comes to spending. We see this with large amounts of money, such as brand-new cars for sixteenth birthdays, monthly purchases of very expensive designer clothes, and unlimited money for concerts and other wants and desires. However, most people don't have this luxury. In the majority of cases, parents who give their kids money for regular little things give kids the message that things are given, not earned. The sooner a child learns the value of money management the better.

Think about how many teenagers have phones that require monthly payments. Most teens know their parents pay for them, but how many know how much they cost? They just take it for granted that the phone will work each month. The apps that are added to their phones or devices can also cost money, but that expense is charged to a parent's credit card, so the teens typically don't know how much they are really spending. Also, consider the number of teens who buy a regular Starbucks drink or go out to eat with friends every day after school. This money adds up very quickly, but teenagers have no idea what the sum total of these purchases is.

We highly recommend that parents teach children and teens about the value of a dollar by sharing with them the costs of things that they are purchasing for their children. It is very important to share things, such as the phone bill, the amount of the extra charge for data usage, and the amount of money that was spent on add-ons, such as apps, songs, movies, and everything else one can purchase for and via a cell phone. Then compare that amount to the number of hours a person would need to work at a minimum wage job for $7.25 per hour to pay those fees.

If during the early years of your children's childhood, you missed the opportunity to teach the lessons that are emphasized in this book, money provides a powerful incentive to learn these lessons, no matter the age of your teenager or young adult. You are in charge of how much you give them and under what circumstances. You set the limit, and when it runs out, it runs out. Teenagers and young adults learn the best from natural consequences, and having a limit to money is a wonderful control mechanism. Let's take the following scenarios we have frequently encountered:

- A teenager shows up late because he was using his debit card to get food on the way to the appointment, but when he went to pay, his card was declined.
- A teen girl used her clothes allowance to buy expensive sunglasses, but then had no more money that month to replace physical education (PE) clothes that she lost, so she had to wear the "borrowed" PE clothes provided by the school.
- A college student used her monthly allowance to eat out every day rather than pack a lunch before class, so she ran out of money by the middle of the month.
- A young man didn't budget his monthly allowance, so he didn't have any left when he asked a girl out on a date.

Consequences for Unauthorized Spending

Children and teenagers should never be given access to their parents' money. They should never be given a credit card or debit card that the parent is responsible for paying. Some families decide to provide an "emergency card" that should only be used for things such as car breakdowns, medical emergencies, or with a parent's permission for a specific reason. For all other spending they can be given an arranged amount of cash, a prepaid debit card, or a debit card that they manage on their own. This allows for the opportunity to learn from natural consequences if they mismanage their money.

Natural Consequences

Natural consequences are those that are not imposed by the parents, but are outcomes that follow money spending. For example, the merchants tell them they don't have the money if their cards are declined, not the parents. When an event comes up and they are not able to participate because they didn't manage their money well, it is their bank account that will tell them no. For teens in this generation who are used to getting things quickly and without planning, this can be a powerful experience. In addition, it takes away the power struggle and arguments with parents because their parents were not the ones who declined them.

Imposed Consequences

Parents ask us all the time what they should do when their children spend money that is not authorized.

First, preview what will happen if your child spends your money without your permission. Nowadays children and teens need accounts with an attached debit or credit card to even use their own funds online. For example, if a kid wants to redeem an iTunes gift card, it needs to be attached to an account with a card on file—typically her parents'. When the amount on the gift card runs out, the child still has access to the account and can spend her mom's or dad's money. Very often kids don't think their "small" purchases even have an effect. Children and teens need to know the limitations of any spending in connection to their parents' money. They also need to know that permission is necessary anytime they spend their parents' money, including things for purchase on a computer, video game, or phone that is paid for with their parents' debit or credit card.

Second, set the consequences.

- Show your child the total amount that was "taken" from you.
- Require your child to pay back all that was spent. If he does not have the money, set up jobs to do to earn the money. Make the hourly wage equivalent to a minimum wage job. Earning the money should not be easy. For example, your child should not be given a dollar for taking the garbage out one time that takes two minutes. Instead, it is five dollars for taking it out once per day for a week. Also, he doesn't get a choice about whether this is worth it. You get to choose how he pays you back. If you don't mind taking out the garbage, but you don't like doing laundry, then have your child do the laundry. Remember, he took the money from you. Therefore, you get to decide.
- Depending on the intention to spend the money, consequences about future money and allowance should be set. If she accidentally purchased an app for a minimum amount, the consequence would not be nearly what it would be if she purposefully hid the spending and spent a larger amount on something that broke established family rules.
- Under no circumstance should your child get any additional money from you until the full amount is paid off.

Balancing Multiple Responsibilities

One of the best things you can do to help your budding young adult is teach him to manage multiple responsibilities at the same time—the juggling act. This means making sure he is responsible for school and extracurricular activities, as well as things such as laundry, preparing meals, and running errands for the family. You will want to introduce these extra responsibilities gradually, but it is important that this becomes an expectation.

By the time adolescents are in their last years of high school, they are used to following a structured schedule of school and extracurricular activities. However, most don't yet have the practice with balancing the other things that are typically taken care of by their parents. Yet this practice is so important in preparing them for the time when they are not at home and this luxury disappears.

We hear from parents all the time that the last two years of high school are so busy for their child that there is no time for them to do the "extra" things. True, those last two years are very busy with prepping for SAT or ACT exams and completing college applications. In fact, that is what makes it the best time to make sure there are additional everyday things for them to be attending to at that same time. Not only is it the time that their brains are ready to develop these connections (see chapter 5), but it is also what they will be expected to do only a year or two later post high school. If they do not practice now, when will they get the practice?

Reinforce the Idea of Considering Others

Older teens and young adults need to be included in the household responsibilities. This not only teaches the organization and planning required for adult life, but it reminds them that they are part of a family unit and they need to consider other people as they are making their way through life. They need to know that they are a valuable and needed member of the group and that their contribution really helps out the family.

As teens get older, their lives do truly become very busy. In fact, there will be periods that they just don't have the time to maintain all the family responsibilities while taking care of their personal responsibilities. This is a perfect time to teach your budding young adult how to ask for help, not expect to be rescued. "Hey, Mom, I have to study for a test and finish a project. Can you please wash my PE clothes for me?" We all need help at times, and it is perfectly OK to support your children by helping them out. In fact, it keeps your relationship strong in the tumultuous teen years. You can also model this by doing the same thing. If you are really busy and could use help getting dinner started, with laundry, or to pick up some things at the store, you should feel very comfortable asking your children for assistance. Not only are they a big help, but it gives you great reasons to give them a lot of positive praise for being responsible and mature.

Does My Child Have a Problem with Procrastination, or Is He Not Ready to Launch?

I was working with a sixteen-year-old boy who was in his sophomore year of high school. His mother called me because she was wondering about school placements for her son. She shared that he was not in the right school because two of his teachers were "horrible." It turned out this boy had a habit of taking between twelve and fifteen "mental health days" per semester. His mother said that he gets really tired with all the pressure and can't do the work at school, but could at home where he was relaxed. When this began, the school would provide her with the work and the boy would do it at home. Once he reached tenth grade, two of his teachers stopped responding to Mom's requests. They said the boy needed to contact them and get the work himself. This made her very angry and she changed her son's school. She thought that fixed the problem, so she didn't need to bring her son in to see me anymore. Fast-forward to his senior year and Mom called again. She said that her son did not start any of his college applications and she needed help because she could not do them all herself.

—Dr. Darlene

Just because a student has the academic record to get accepted into a choice college does not mean that student is ready to take on the responsibility required to be a successful college student. On multiple occasions, we have received calls from a parent whose child successfully graduated from high school and was accepted into a school of her choice. After the first semester or two, the student wanted to come home. The experience was not what she expected, she was feeling overwhelmed with the academic challenges, or she was having difficulty socially or with living in a dorm or apartment. Some parents try to find excuses, such as "The school was not a good fit," or "There was a bad roommate situation." But the fact was that most often, the student was just not prepared.

Is It Just Procrastination?

> **Parent:** Dr. Sweetland, we need your help. It is November and Sue has not begun her college applications yet.

Completing college applications can be a very daunting prospect for most teenagers. In fact, most students need the support from the adults around them to figure out how to organize the information and set a plan about collecting all the materials and completing each application. If you have a child who is prone to procrastination, you will likely see it during this process.

At the same time, if you have a child who is not ready to take on the challenge of a four-year college away from home, he or she is likely to cover it up by making it appear to be procrastination. So how do you know the difference?

Signs of Procrastination

- The child waits until the last minute to complete work.
- The child has a plan and assumes it will go smoothly, even if it is not a well-thought-out plan.
- The child exhibits poor time management.

- The child misses out on activities because he has to finish projects.
- The child experiences increased stress because there was not a comfortable amount of time to complete something.
- The child fails to account for unexpected delays in work completion (e.g., computer froze, printer broke, discovered an instruction he or she wasn't prepared for).

Notice that students who procrastinate have a plan and assume they have enough time to follow their plan. These are students who are confident that they have left themselves enough time to complete the work and rationalize this at each step when they put off doing it. They just tend to underestimate the amount of time it will take to complete tasks and they don't account for unexpected things happening so they end up scrambling to finish things at the last minute.

Red Flags That Your Child May Not Be Ready

- The teenager shows little interest in researching, hearing about, or visiting colleges.
- The teenager needs constant parent reminders to work on college applications.
- The teenager tells you, "I know! I will do it!" but never does.
- The teenager requires an adult to help with each step of the application process, otherwise does not work on the applications at all.
- The teenager won't pass a class in her or his senior year without the parents' assistance.
- The teenager has no way to get all the work done to

complete the applications in time without a lot of help from others.

- The teenager shows signs of anxiety when the topic is discussed.

Notice that there is a sense of resistance with students who aren't ready. Parents tend to feel panicked and try to force the matter, but these students are often just not ready. We repeatedly hear from parents that they need to help their children through their senior year, because they think that once the young person is at college the goal is achieved. In fact, most often if the student is not ready, he or she does not make it through the first year. The student then leaves college, feeling like a failure, and must figure out what to do next. When the red flags are there, other options need to be considered, as well.

Discuss All the Options

Going to college is a privilege, not a right. This needs to be clearly communicated to students, and the application process is the perfect time to do so. Once students know that going to college is not a done deal, they usually kick it into gear and take more responsibility if they are truly ready for it.

Therefore, discuss all the options for when he graduates from high school. Discuss how the parents will and will not support the child if he goes away to college, goes to a local college, or gets a job. This makes it clear that going away to college is only one option.

How to Prepare Young Adults for What Is Expected after Graduation

Whether you have a child who is ready to take on the world or one who has been hampered by the challenges of the Instant Gratification Generation, it is very important for teens to know what is expected of them as young adults. They are going to be making many choices about the direction they take in life, and it is important that they know there are consequences based on those choices, both positive and negative.

Establish a Monthly Allowance

If your child is heading to a four-year residential college and living in the dorms, the first thing you need to decide is whether she will be getting a monthly allowance, and if so, how much it will be. Under no circumstances should any young adult have an open-ended credit card that is paid for by their parents. Living in the dorms is a great transitional move in this regard because all the expenses of room and board are wrapped together into the school's tuition, room, and board bill. Therefore, you know your child will have a place to live and access to food, even if he or she runs out of spending money.

One of the most common complaints from parents about the transition away from home is about money. This complaint is even more frequent when their children are not required to budget. Let's consider monthly allowance. The amount you decide on should be limited and force your child to budget. The key is to "require" your child to budget. Virtually, all the parents we work with tell their children they need to be careful about their spending and talk with them about the necessity of keeping a budget, but that doesn't stop the spending. Parents need to set a limit and stick to it. When their children begin to complain that it is not enough or that they miss out on things because they don't have the money, tell them to "figure it out." They will need to decide how to adjust their spending. For example, will they shop less so they can go out more or eat in the cafeteria at the dorms for free (even pack a lunch for later on campus) so they don't spend money on food?

Set Grade Expectations

Students need to know before they begin college what the expectations are around grades. Parents need to be very specific. For example, do they need to maintain a C (maybe B, you know your child) or better in every class? Students need to be reminded that going to college is a privilege. Not everyone attends college, and those who are there need to continue to earn it.

Many students approach college as a way to postpone getting a job. They need to understand before starting college that succeeding there *is* their job and with it comes expectations. Just as with any job, there are going to be challenges and students are going to need help and guidance to deal with those challenges. For example, college coursework is often really difficult. If there is a class that is particularly challenging and there is a risk of the student not meeting the expectation you've set for them, they need to have a conversation with you. And it needs to happen early in the semester, not at the end when they realize they didn't pass the class. Just as employees will go to their boss when they are asked to complete a task they don't know how to do, college students need to talk with their parents about their challenges and propose solutions to make it better. Here is an example.

> *"Hey, Dad, I just took my first math test and got a D. Math has always been hard for me and I am really worried*

about this class. I went to the student center to find out about tutoring. They offer some great services but they aren't free. Would you be able to pay for a tutor so I can pass this class?"

Set an expectation that when problems arise, your children must deal with them responsibly and communicate with you accordingly. Then if he or she does not meet your academic expectations, it is not a surprise and you were informed of the ways he or she was taking responsibility. The expectation is not for your children to be perfect students. It is for them to be responsible students. You will find that if you make this clear and have a sample conversation before your child even leaves for college, he or she will be much more open about grades during the semester.

What to Do If Your Child Is Just Not Ready

One afternoon, I received a frantic message from the mother of an eleventh-grade student. It was flagged "urgent." When I called back, she shared that her son was going to earn a C in his literature class because he still had not turned in a paper that was a major portion of the grade. She had called the teacher to explain that he was working on it the night before and would complete it that day. The teacher responded that her son had several weeks to complete the paper and that the class had already been given a three-day extension. He would not accept the late paper from her son. That was when she called me to ask that I write a letter stating that he should be granted another extension. She told me that he would never get into a "good school," meaning college, because he was going to have a C on his transcript.

—Dr. Darlene

Experiencing the consequences of making a mistake is essential in helping children and teens learn how to solve problems. Failing to turn the paper in on time could be the result of many things; maybe he did not have the skills to organize himself or he simply did not care about the grade. Either way, it may have been one of many indications that he was not ready to attend an academically challenging college. In fact, despite the tragic C in literature, three years later he was attending a four-year university and I received another call from his mother stating that he was failing his classes and was overdrawing the savings account his parents set up for him. She did not know why he was acting so irresponsibly and wanted my help.

That same week I met with parents of a twelfth-grade student. They said their daughter was earning a D in a history class because she hadn't completed some assignments. The teacher met with this girl and offered her an extension, but she still wasn't doing the work. Her parents were very concerned about what the grade would do to her GPA and her college prospects. They wanted me to call and talk with the teacher. My response was, "She should get a D because that is what she earned. If, as a senior, she needs this much support to complete some work that is easy for her, then she might be showing you she is not ready to do it on her own."

—Dr. Darlene

If you have a child who is not ready to follow the path to a four-year university right out of high school, there are many options for students to receive higher education. Many parents get stuck on the idea that a traditional four-year college education is the only option after high school graduation. They fear that if their children don't go directly to a four-year institution, the motivation for college will disappear altogether. In fact, there are a lot of resourceful ways to maintain the motivation for higher education.

The first, and most important, thing to do when talking to young adults about higher education is to talk about the options with enthusiasm. Do not present the options with a sense of resignation or disappointment in your voice, such as "Well, if you don't go to a four-year college, you will have to go to a community college." This makes it sound like it is a weak choice, and that will really dampen any student's motivation and excitement about their prospects.

The second requirement is to identify what they are emotionally, developmentally, and educationally ready for when they graduate from high school. Every college campus is different and each environment offers a different set of supports. It is important to find one that meets the student's needs. Consider the following factors when assessing what type of environment is best for your child.

Educational Readiness

- What type of academic rigor would be best?
- Might the student need academic support, such as a strong learning center or peer mentor program?
- Is the student looking to be challenged and can she take on

difficult academic work, but didn't have the grades to get into the college of her choice at that time?

Maturational Readiness

- Does the student need parental support and would he do best close to home?
- Even though the student isn't ready for the academic work of a four-year college, does he or she need to move away from home to mature?
- How much structure is needed in the student's environment to be successful?
- Will the transition be more successful if the student doesn't have to worry about room and board (living in a dorm and all the structure that entails might be a great thing)?

Social Readiness

- Would the student do better in a structured social environment, such as a dorm?
- Is the student social and able to make connections at a commuter school, or would a more traditional college environment be better?
- Will it be important to find a school with a student mentor program?
- Is the student looking for a school with activities such as football games, clubs, and organizations?

Once the student's wishes and needs are identified, if a student isn't ready for a rigorous four-year university consider the different educational options. Here are just a few:

- **Small Four-Year College with Mandatory Dorm Residency:** There are small four-year colleges that provide a lot of support for students who need it. They tend to have small class size, and living on campus is mandatory for all the years they attend. This keeps things structured for the student.
- **Community College with a Dorm:** This option allows the student to go away to school and have the dorm experience, which is very normalizing. These programs also tend to have good transfer programs with the more traditional four-year colleges following completion of the two-year program. This is a great option for students who did not receive the grades required to get into the college of their choice. It allows them to get away and experience college, earn the same college credits, and the option to transfer when they are ready.
- **Community College with Certificate Programs:** It is highly recommended that students are encouraged to choose a community college that has a certificate in an area of interest to them. This will heighten their motivation to attend school, as well as give them something to work toward as they are gaining general education credits. If they earn a certificate on their way to an associate degree, they have something to fall back on if they decide that they really don't want to continue in college.

  For students who really do not want to attend a school where they have to take the mandatory lower division courses to earn a degree, a certificate program at a community college can be a great option. They can choose a school that has a certificate in a professional field of their choice. There are certificates programs in almost any field of study. If the student decides she would like to pursue an associate degree or a bachelor's degree, it is easy to transfer those credits. This is a great option for students who don't know what they want to do or if they even want to complete a bachelor's degree.

- **Technical Schools:** Technical schools can be a great option for students who know exactly what they want to do and don't need a bachelor's degree to do it. One student may want to be a veterinary technician, while another may want to go to design school. Encourage the student to identify the career path or area of interest, research the requirements, and create a plan to reach that goal.

Remember, the goal for this generation of emerging adults is to help them plan ahead, make considerate choices, and, ultimately, *to think*. We want to discourage a reaction of resignation when they don't think of a solution right away or if they find their path is different than what they expected. The high school senior in the previous vignette decided to attend a community college with a culinary arts certificate. She also found a school with a dormitory so that she can move away from home and experience independent college life. Before leaving for college, she shared that she was excited about her program and said, "Who knows? I think I might want to get a bachelor's degree after all." Either way, she is receiving higher education with a goal.

The message for young adults is that almost any goal is achievable. There may just be a different road to get there than what they expected.

Putting It All Together

The Issue

Families have been talking about life after high school for a long time. When September rolls around in your child's senior year of high school, the questions about general plans after graduation become much more specific. Parents dream of this time as being one of pride as they share with their friends what college their child will attend and what their major will be. It causes a lot of discomfort when the answer is not so clear or nonexistent.

The Trap

Many parents have ideas of what they expect their children to do after they graduate high school, and this is the time for them to see if their child followed the path they wanted him to follow. When the answer is not so clear, parents feel the need to make excuses or push their child into college even when they are not ready or don't want to go. There is a push to make up what the "plan" is if their children aren't sure.

The Alternative

Be honest with yourself and allow your child to be honest with you about what he or she is truly prepared for after graduation. Remember, the goal is to raise children to be responsible, conscientious, and self-sufficient adults. There are many wonderful paths to reach that goal. Make sure that you are communicating that to your children. Teach them to think by being conscientious about identifying a goal, researching a plan to meet that goal, and identifying ways to fulfill that plan.

Whatever your child's plan is, make sure the expectations for them in regards to money management and grades is clear ahead of time. Then tell them ahead of time what the consequences will be if they do not meet their responsibilities.

CHAPTER 12

Parents Have Grown Accustomed to Instant Gratification Too

We are all becoming accustomed to the rapid pace of our culture. I find myself getting very impatient with the computer when I am working in more than one program at a time. If I try to enter something and the computer doesn't respond quickly, I tend to push so many buttons that the whole thing freezes up in revolt.

—Dr. Darlene

Part of the reinforcement for instant gratification for children and teens is that parents get caught up in the phenomenon too. Think of the frustration you feel when a video is buffering or there is a weak Wi-Fi connection. We usually react with surprise and frustration. Waiting even a minute can seem like forever. If right now you pause and observe the seconds pass on your watch for a minute, you will actually see how long that feels.

As adults, we also have become accustomed to an onslaught of information anytime we want it. Not only do we appreciate our computers and smartphones because they allow us to stay up to date on current events, emails, and the news, but we also use them as a quick and efficient way to tackle interpersonal communication. It is very easy for adults to get caught up in the social media frenzy. This activity can consume several hours in a day. Many adults have told us that they have canceled their social media accounts because it was taking up so much free time. They could not stop themselves from checking it continuously.

Because this drive for things to happen quickly is so infused into our culture, it is particularly important for parents to be aware of how they inadvertently support instant gratification as an expectation in their children.

Have Patience

Does the following scenario sound familiar?

> *A parent interrupts a conversation with you to read a text from her child. She is distracted with the text conversation and then talks about what problem the child wants solved until receiving another text that there was a resolution.*

The temptation for parents to jump in to rescue their children from problems can often be due to a lack of patience on the parents' part. In fact, solving a child's problem quickly can feel like a relief to parents. You probably recognize the foregoing scenario in yourself, others, or both. Texting offers such an easy and immediate avenue to get solutions to your children. In this way, a quick reply with a solution, or even suggestion, reinforces instant gratification in both children and their parents.

Very often, a parent gets caught in the rescue trap because the *parent* has a hard time waiting. Many times children and teens come to their parents with a complaint about something that is happening in their life. It takes a lot of patience to be a good listener, not offer any suggestions, and, ultimately, avoid the rescue trap. It would be much easier to offer advice or tell them what to do. Yet this not only takes away opportunities for them to solve problems and find solutions on their own, but it also communicates to them that problems should be solved quickly.

Have Patience with Text Messaging

Parents have a hard time delaying responses to text messages from their kids too. However, there are times when you shouldn't respond immediately, such as when you are at an appointment, social event, or personal activity. Your children should know that you are not going to reply right away during these times. Text messages are an option for contact, not a guarantee.

Therefore, make it a rule to wait before replying to a text. If you are in a meeting, spending time with a friend, or taking time for yourself, don't break away from that to answer a text immediately. Even though it is tempting, remember part of the temptation is your need for instant action. Don't deprive your children of the practice building tolerance for waiting because you want immediate action.

Then clarify times when your kids need to know that you are available to them. For example, assure them that you will reply promptly to texts if they are home alone, driving somewhere on their own, or you know they will need your permission for something. During those times, it is great to agree on when you will be available for a text message or phone call if they need you.

Be Aware of the Messages You Send

You know the saying, "Do as I say, not as I do," meaning "Don't imitate my behavior, just obey my instructions." Sometimes parents inadvertently give their child mixed messages that, as a result, actually support or teach undesirable behaviors to children. For example, parents regularly share with us that they want their children to be polite and show good manners, such as not interrupting when a parent is on the phone. The parent may say, "Don't interrupt me. I am on the phone" several times to no avail. Even though the parent is getting increasingly frustrated with the child, the child continues to pester. The parent then falls into the hurried trap, gives in, and quickly answers the child's question so they can continue their conversation. This teaches children that their parent's frustration does not matter. Instead, children learn that if they persist, they get what they want. Children will see their own needs as more important than the needs of others, and their desire for instant gratification is supported.

In my waiting room, I observed the following scenario. A mother was on her cell phone and her son was interrupting her because he wanted the Wi-Fi password for his iPod Touch. She asked him to wait and he proceeded to become frustrated with her, pull on her arm, and ask louder for the Wi-Fi password. The mother asked the person she was talking with to please wait and quietly gave her son the password. She finished her phone call and, just as quietly, took his iPod, told him he would not be able to use it until after the weekend, and not to interrupt her when she is on the phone. She maintained her composure for the person on the phone, but her actions clearly communicated to her son that interrupting her was not acceptable. I don't intervene with scenarios like these because outside of my office, I am not there to step in and they are great teaching moments that we can discuss in the upcoming session. In this case, I learned a great strategy from her.

—Dr. Darlene

Parents also model how to use electronics by their own actions. Adults are often complaining or making jokes about how teenagers always have a phone in their hands. Many parents go so far as to describe it as an "addiction." Parents try to set limits on cell-phone use and break their kids of this habit by telling them it is a distraction and inappropriate. Then those same parents take out their phones to check emails, text messages, and news reports when they are spending time with the family. Pay attention to how many times you check your phone when waiting with your family at a restaurant, at a child's sporting event, or even with kids on a vacation. Parents also need to be watchful of their intolerance for downtime. In the previous example, the child was eager to fill downtime with an electronic device. That mother dealt with it very well, but how often do parents promote the intolerance by modeling it with their own actions?

Children and teens are very picky about which lessons from their parents they choose to follow. Do you think they will do as their parents *say* and decrease the amount of time they spend on their phone or do what their parents *do* and keep the phone close so they can check incoming information constantly?

Allow Yourself to Make Mistakes Too

If you are reading this book, there is a high likelihood that you want to learn tips on how to raise children and teens in the Instant Gratification Generation. That means that you want to support the children in your life in dealing with the unique challenges of this generation. Whether you are coaching, rearing, teaching, or just thinking about kids in this generation, the fact that you are seeking this information shows you care—and that's what matters most. Doing everything "right" as a parent is not realistic. Making a mistake doesn't mean you're not capable.

As we saw in chapter 3, it is important not only for your state of mind but for your children's as well to allow yourself to make mistakes. If you always come off as the expert, they feel they need to be experts too. They will interpret your desire for perfection as a message that it is what you expect of them and you won't be proud of anything less. On the other hand, when they see you make mistakes, they come to be more tolerant with their own mistakes.

In addition, children need to see you struggle with some things because they can really benefit from seeing adults deal with mistakes openly. This gives them opportunities to observe how you deal with the frustration and then how you pull it together to solve problems.

A very common mistake parents make with their children is impulsively giving them a consequence for something they did that they later realize is either too lenient or too strict. It is a very common issue and one that can be addressed while teaching children an important lesson, because we all know they react to their emotions impulsively too.

Take the scenario of a parent reacting in anger by giving a consequence that is too strict. For example, a child disrespects his parent in the grocery store and the parent tells the child she will lose electronics for a month. The parent later realizes that a month is probably too long for the punishment, so starts acquiescing after a couple of days and lets the child use electronics a little more each day. Instead of giving the child mixed messages by trying to cover the mistake, parents need to talk with their children about their thoughts.

> *"Joe, I was so angry in the store because you were being disrespectful to me, but I reacted too strongly. When I got home, I realized that losing your electronics for a month was an exaggerated reaction. I made a mistake and I am changing it to a week."*

Alternately, if you realize that the consequence you set was too lenient you can also make that clear to your children.

> *"Jane, I know I said you would only lose electronics for the weekend, but when I got home I remembered that the last time you were disrespectful toward me, I told you that you would lose them for a week. Now you will not be able to use electronics for a week."*

This models for kids how to fix a mistake when they react impulsively. It also shows that you are using good reasoning by considering what you said before, and are thoughtful in how you choose to respond to their behavior. This is exactly how you want them to react to others.

All parents make mistakes. Don't feel like you are going to read this book, or any other, and do everything that is suggested all the time. Just as you want to teach your children to be thoughtful and considerate when they approach life's challenges, mistakes and all, you need to give yourself the same benefit.

The Pressure to Keep Up

The pace of our society is very fast. Some people really thrive in this fast pace and others prefer it a little slower and feel overwhelmed by it. Just as with anything else, each person experiences it differently. This is true for parents as well as their children.

The ease with which we are able to communicate and share information has significantly increased the pressure parents feel to involve their children in every activity. Parents can't help but compare themselves against other parents who talk, send emails, or post on social media about their children's activities, programs, and academic success. This kind of information sharing can be helpful and positive, but think about the sheer variety and number of programs parents are hearing about today. If your child plays a sport, you get all the information on off-season practice and league play. If your child attended a camp, you get information about all the other programs the camp offers, and if you had any communication with an agency about your child, you now get emails from all the sister agencies. This can be extremely overwhelming and cause parents to doubt that they are doing enough for their children, which leads to anxiety.

It is very important for parents to be aware of how they deal with the sense of feeling overwhelmed, which children easily pick up on. Some children are energized by all the opportunities available to them, while others are anxious and stressed. Each child is different, and parents need to be aware of when their own response to the pressure is the driving force.

This is a very provocative time in our culture. Things are easy, rapidly evolving, and the advancements in technology are mind blowing. That is what makes falling into the traps of the Instant Gratification Generation so alluring. It happens without us even knowing it. If it is so easy for adults to be lured into the traps, imagine how easy it is for children and teens to fall into this way of life.

Putting It All Together

The Issue

The progressive advancements and conveniences of today's culture are so amazing. It's easy to get caught up in the excitement of new ways to stay connected, get information, and deal with everyday problems.

The Trap

Because instant access to everything is so infused in our culture, most parents don't even realize they are acting with impatience. All the new technological developments and ways to get information are fun and entertaining. At the same time, it is so easy to get caught up in the wave of fast and easy, that this readily gets passed on to our children. Parents begin to model the exact patterns that they want their children to avoid.

The Alternative

The most important thing for parents to do is recognize it when they are getting caught up in the rip current of the fast pace and push toward instant gratification of this culture. Step back and look for everyday opportunities to slow down. This has been the way of life for most children and teens, so they are unaware of the opportunities they are missing or the poor habits that are being developed.

Therefore, parents are going to need to slow the pace for them. In doing so, it means they need to have more patience and remain self-aware of their own tendencies to support the immediacy that is rampant in this generation.

There are many children who will express stress or anxiety related to the pressure they feel when trying to keep up with the pace. The following are signs of anxiety:

- Your child says regularly that he is not good enough or feeling inadequate.
- Your child talks about being "tired" all the time.
- Your child consistently compares herself with others.
- Your child is a good student, but is anxious that his performance is not good enough.
- Your child begins to miss school because she is run-down and needs the day off.

It is very important for parents to be aware of the signs that this may be occurring for their children. The next step is for the parent to closely examine what they may be doing or communicating that encourages such a fast pace and take steps to balance accomplishments and reasonable expectations.

CHAPTER 13
Lessons Learned

Throughout this book, we have talked a lot about how the Instant Gratification Generation is at a considerable disadvantage when it comes to learning the wide variety of skills that are so important throughout childhood and into adulthood. Instant gratification is encouraged in so many aspects of their lives. Today's kids expect things to happen quickly, they have fewer daily opportunities to practice solving problems, and the pressures to excel at both school and extracurricular activities can be overwhelming. For this final chapter, let's briefly review the most common parenting traps and summarize the key recommendations that will help you take a more active approach to parenting, which will increase your children's ability to think, solve problems, and develop a healthy level of self-confidence. The goal is to raise *confident, independent, and thoughtful children.*

The Traps
Remember from chapter 1 that a *parent trap* is a situation in which parents are drawn to solve problems or rescue their

children in a way that ultimately stifles growth opportunities for their children. Every parent is faced with these situations on an almost daily basis. However, by understanding the trap and developing a plan to avoid it, a parent is setting her child up to be in a great position to take on a childhood full of opportunity.

The Rescue Trap

This is probably the most common trap we see parents encounter. Parents hate to see their children struggle at anything or be unhappy. As a result, parents often save their children from this experience by fixing their problems for them, as fast as possible. It makes sense at the time and doesn't feel like there would be any consequence to doing it. However, the more it happens, the more likely a child is to expect it. The consequence of this parental behavior is the child's learned expectation that things will be done for him and that he doesn't have the opportunity to learn to solve the problem himself.

The Hurried Trap

Parents want to do everything in their power for their children and that includes feeling pushed to meet their needs quickly. A prominent issue with the Instant Gratification Generation is the reluctance of our children and adolescents to wait for things. Even the simple act of waiting tends to create anxiety and uncertainty with children today and this is something that parents find difficult to watch, especially when they have it in their power to relieve the anxiety. It ends up that parents are pretty good at solving their children's problems quickly. Probably because it is usually fairly easy to do and has such an immediate impact on a child's happiness, it happens a lot. However, in doing so, they enable a pattern of instant gratification.

The Pressure Trap

All parents feel proud sharing their children's accomplishments. There is a consistent message to parents from school, coaches, family, and other parents that children should perform at the highest levels possible in each area of their lives. Parents work to help their children to be at the top of the class, the best player on a team, and have the most friends. Parents want their children to feel confident and good about themselves so they encourage extra enrichment to push their kids ahead. Societal expectations have driven many parents to question if they are doing enough to provide every possible opportunity for their child. Often the result of all this good intention is a child who is overscheduled and has very little free time to be a kid and deal with a child's problems. In addition, many children are pushed past their optimal developmental level, which becomes very overwhelming and can cause insecurity. The pressure trap often starts the day you know you are going to have a baby, but it is never too late to incorporate a healthy balance into both your life and your child's life.

The Giving Trap

Many parents have dreamt of being able to give their children everything they want, and parents certainly don't want their children to feel different. The result is that parents fall in the trap of giving material items that their kids didn't have to work for. We constantly marvel at the number of kids we interact with who have new smartphones, toys, and the latest fashions received as a matter of course rather than for some special occasion. When children get things without working for them, it plays right into the culture of instant gratification.

The Guilt Trap

Guilt is a very real issue in parenting. Parents don't ever want to be the cause for their child's unhappiness. Whether it is setting a limit or not giving in to a request, parents know they played a part when their child is upset. Often this guilt is self-imposed by the parent, and other times it is enhanced by the child's pleas. Either way, it is very tempting to give in to the guilt and give the child what he or she wants. In addition, in today's culture, families are extremely busy and often parents are working more hours. When parents feel guilty that they are disappointing their children because they are not available, they tend to overindulge their children to make up for it. This is bound to happen from time to time, but when it is established as an expectation of the child, it becomes a problem. It is actually developmentally normal for kids to try to make their parents feel guilty so they can get more things. It is the parent's job to identify the trap and implement a productive parenting strategy.

To this point we have focused on the traps that parents routinely face. Identifying the traps is an important component of making positive changes in one's parenting. The following section will address specific strategies to help with this change.

Positive Parenting Strategies

For this final chapter we would like to summarize the key recommendations that were integrated in different ways in each chapter of the book to provide an easy reference for the reader. The following strategies are the ones we have found to be the most effective from our work with hundreds of families over the last two decades.

Celebrate the Opportunity for Challenges

Things are easier for this generation. They get things quicker, have more aides to solve problems for them, and they clearly experience far fewer everyday inconveniences or challenges than past generations. While this sounds great, it means that they are also missing out. They are missing out on opportunities to practice solving problems and experiences to build their self-confidence. They are entering adulthood vastly underprepared because they have been *taught not to think*.

As discussed in depth throughout this book, the technological advances and pressures on parents have only reinforced the need for instant gratification. In addition, the conveniences of this generation are very alluring. They make it so easy for parents to rescue their children and take away times of frustration. In fact, things are only going to get easier in this regard. We too celebrate this time in our lives. But in order for children and teens to gain the experience necessary to tackle the challenges of adulthood, they need to experience challenges throughout their childhood.

We would like parents to rethink the way they view their children's trials and tribulations. We ask that parents celebrate them as an opportunity to practice using the skills that will be essential throughout the rest of their lives. Celebrate the mistakes and learn important information about your children as you watch them solve their problems.

Integrate Waiting at Each Age

For all the reasons discussed throughout this book, the Instant Gratification Generation is inundated with the expectation that things come easily and quickly to them. This is supported by the culture of technology, but it can be countered by parents.

Parents often talk to us about their concern with the challenges of this generation and are exasperated with not knowing what to do. Our first response is almost always to integrate waiting into their everyday experience. Because our culture is so infused with things that come quickly it is up to the parents to support waiting by providing daily opportunities for their children.

Waiting can be integrated into the daily lives of children of all ages. When a person is required to wait, it allows him to be thoughtful of his actions, observant of his environment, and considerate of others. It also gives him an opportunity to think. Many kids actually get anxious if they have to wait even a few seconds. If waiting becomes part of their everyday experience, they develop those personal qualities to tolerate and maybe even take advantage of it. If it does not, the transition into the adult world where those qualities are required can be quite difficult. The earlier you start the better.

Here are just a few simple ways to introduce waiting:

- More often than not, ask your child to wait when he asks you for those daily things, such as something to eat, to wash specific clothes, a ride, and so on. Toddlers can wait thirty seconds to two minutes for a snack or TV show, and teens can wait as long as you need them to.
- Never buy your child something in the store when something simply catches her interest. This sets up a strong pattern of immediate gratification.
- Always have your children work for extra things they may want. They can work for it and earn money or they can earn "credit" toward the item.
- Resist the temptation to soothe your child with an electronic device every time he has to wait for something. Let him figure out other ways to pass the time while he waits.

Help Children See They Are Part of a Family Unit

For children and teens to be conscientious and considerate as individuals, community members, and employees, they need to be aware of the people around them. Teachers, administrators, and coaches that we interviewed consistently listed social skills, awareness of others, and overall "people skills" as being some of the top characteristics they see in a successful student, athlete, and young adult.

Part of having great social skills is having an awareness of others around you. For some children this comes naturally, but others need to be taught and practice. One way to teach this is by helping your children see that they are part of the family unit. This means that all family members are considered when decisions are made.

Think of the difference between the teen who says, "Mom, I need you to drive me to Jane's tonight" versus "Mom, do you have time to give me a ride to Jane's tonight?" If Mom lets the teen know she has other plans that night and can't drive her, the first teen is likely to get angry and perhaps also frustrated. On the other hand, the second teen is likely to try to solve the problem with her mom. She considered the circumstances of her mother as well as herself, which is the core of being a part of the family unit.

Focus on the Process over the Product

The pressures parents feel for their children to achieve is so strong for this generation. The comparisons that occur between families, students, and athletes occur frequently. The result is an emphasis on objective things, such as grades, trophies, and awards instead of the work a child may put toward meeting a goal.

Parents tend to gravitate toward the objective things because they are concrete, measurable, and easy to talk about. On the other hand, it is the work, planning, and effort a child puts toward achieving a goal that offers them practice in developing the skills discussed in this book and is the core of *Teaching Kids to Think*. In fact, children who struggle and learn how to overcome and compensate for challenges develop stronger life skills and resiliency than those who achieve things easily. The work needs to be celebrated even more than the outcome.

Teach Them to Work for It

Because so many things come easily to children and teens in this generation, it is easy to see how they get used to getting things without working for them. They develop a very low frustration tolerance when things don't go as expected.

We believe in the idea of earning things over getting things. Even young children can be taught that they need to help with tasks to earn things they want. It is sometimes helpful to think of these "things" (toys, video games, clothes, smartphones) as goals. Based on the age of your child, you can help him develop a way to meet his goal or you can ask him to present you with a plan to meet his goal. Kids can earn money or credit by helping around the house, saving money, doing extra work at home, improving their effort at school, or even by showing progress in an aspect of their life that they are working on.

The bottom line is that most things hold more meaning when they are earned than when they are given for no apparent reason. Birthdays, holidays, and other special occasions are plenty of opportunity to give things to our children as unearned gifts. Maybe the best gift you can give them is the knowledge that they can make a plan to get the special things they want all by themselves.

Teaching Kids to Think

Teaching Kids to Think: Raising Confident, Independent, and Thoughtful Children in an Age of Instant Gratification is the result of decades of meaningful work with great families. We hope you find our explanation of common parent traps useful and that by following some of our specific suggestions you help your kids achieve their goals and prepare them to take on the world. By providing specific strategies for a wide variety of childhood issues, it is our hope that you found something that applies to your family.

Acknowledgments

It goes without saying that countless people have contributed to this project in ways that they may never know. Sometimes we needed the little things like simple words of encouragement and a gentle nudge to keep working. Other times we needed someone to bounce ideas off of or insights into the scary world of publishing. To all of you we offer a heartfelt thank-you.

None of this would have been possible without the amazing families that we work with. They come to our office looking for support, and in that process, they share their secrets, fears, and worries. It is said that asking for help is one of the hardest things to do, so we thank the brave families that have let us into their lives and asked for help.

We interviewed many teachers, school administrators, coaches, and employers when writing this book. They provided numerous examples and insights about their experiences with the challenges they face with this generation of kids. We are so grateful for their time and expertise in sharing what they know.

They are clearly very passionate and committed to raising children to be confident, independent, and thoughtful.

We also need to thank Donna Pinto. Donna is an accomplished author and editor in her own right, and we greatly value her opinion and critical edit of our work. She helped us organize our thoughts, and as she read our work, she gave us confidence that we were on the right track.

Family is everything to us. We are both so fortunate to have parents who taught us to dream big. Darryl and Barbara Sweetland and Roger and Mary Stolberg have been a never-ending source of encouragement and support. Our children, Aaron and Drew, have been equally important in this regard, as they remind us daily that being a parent is the greatest job in the world. We are eternally grateful to all of them.

Our agent, Jill Marr, and the entire Sandra Dijkstra Literary Agency has shown such positive enthusiasm about this project from the start. We knew after only a few minutes with Jill that she was the one we wanted representing us and this book. She understood our message and had faith that this book would communicate it well. It has been so comforting to us knowing that she was as committed and passionate about this project as we were.

Finally, none of this would be possible without the fullest support of our editorial director, Shana Drehs, at Sourcebooks Inc. We have no doubt that Shana and her talented team of editors have refined and improved our message in ways we simply could not have done on our own. We are confident that we have the best team working with us to make this project everything we ever dreamt it could be.

Notes

Note: Online resources were most recently accessed in July 2014.

Introduction

1. Joel Stein, "Millennials: The Me Me Me Generation," *Time*, May 20, 2013, http://time.com/247/millennials -the-me-me-me-generation; Mickey Goodman, "Are We Raising a Generation of Helpless Kids?" Huffington Post, www.huffingtonpost.com/Mickey-goodman/are-we-raising -a-generati_b_1249706.html.
2. Yolanda Williams, "The Silent Generation: Definition, Characteristics & Facts," Education-portal.com, http://educa tion-portal.com/academy/lesson/the-silent-generation -definition-characteristics-facts.html#lesson.
3. Gary Gilles, "What Are Baby Boomers?—Definition, Age & Characteristics," Education-portal.com, http://education -portal.com/academy/lesson/what-are-baby-boomers -definition-age-characteristics.html#lesson.
4. Andrea McKay, "Generation X: Definition, Characteristics

& Quiz," Education-portal.com, www.education-portal.com /academy/lesson/generation-x-definition-characteristics -quiz.html#lesson.

5. Chevette Alston, "Generation Y: Definition, Characteristics & Personality Traits," Education-portal.com, www.educa tion-portal.com/academy/lesson/generation-y-definition -characteristics-personality-traits.html#lesson.

6. Candace Sweat, "Expert Says New Generation Wants Instant Gratification. Are Parents to Blame?" Alabama's ABC 33/40, www.abc3340.com/story/17115375/expert-says-new-generation -wants-instant-gratification-are-parents-to-blame.

Chapter 1

1. Walter Mischel and Ebbe B. Ebbesen, "Attention in Delay of Gratification," *Journal of Personality and Social Psychology* 16, no. 2 (1970): 329–37.

2. Yuichi Shoda, Walter Mischel, and Philip K. Peake, "Predicting Adolescent Cognitive and Self-Regulatory Competencies from Preschool Delay of Gratification: Identifying Diagnostic Conditions," *Developmental Psychology* 26, no. 6 (1990): 978–86.

3. Walter Mischel, Yuichi Shoda, and Monica L. Rodriguez, "Delay of Gratification in Children," *Science*, New Series 244, no. 4907 (1989): 933–38.

4. Kevin G. Hall, "Teen Employment Hits Record Lows Suggesting Lost Generation," McClatchy DC, Washington Bureau, www .mcclatchydc.com/2013/08/29/200769/teen-employment -hits-record-lows.html.

Chapter 2

1. Kendra Cherry, "The 4 Stages of Cognitive Development in Young Children," About.com Psychology, http://psychology .about.com/od/piagetstheory/a/keyconcepts.htm.

Chapter 3

1. Kate Bayless, "What Is Helicopter Parenting?" *Parents Magazine*, www.parents.com/parenting/better-parenting/what -is-helicopter-parenting.
2. GypsyNesters, "Are You a Snow Plow Parent? 7 Modern Parenting Terms," Huffington Post, www.huffingtonpost .com/the-gypsynesters/parenting_b_1894237.html.
3. National Center for Safe Routes to School, "How Children Get to School: School Travel Patterns from 1969 to 2009," www.saferoutesinfo.org/sites/default/files/resources/NHTS _school_travel_report_2011_0.pdf.

Chapter 4

1. Erik H. Erikson, *Childhood and Society* (New York: Norton, 1950).
2. Erik H. Erikson, *Identity and the Life Cycle* (New York: Norton, 1980).
3. Jean Piaget, *Biology and Knowledge: An Essay on the Relations between Organic Regulations and Cognitive Processes* (Chicago: University of Chicago Press, 1971).
4. Kendra Cherry, "All about Kohlberg's Theory of Moral Development," About.com Psychology, http://psychology .about.com/od/developmentalpsychology/a/kohlberg.htm.
5. Lawrence Kohlberg, "The Development of Children's Orientations toward a Moral Order: I. Sequence in the Development of Moral Thought," *Human Development* 6, no. 1–2 (1963): 11–33.

Chapter 5

1. Erikson, *Childhood and Society*; Piaget, *Biology and Knowledge.*
2. "Critical Period (Psychology)," Reference.MD.com, www
.reference.md/files/D003/mD003423.html.
3. Jacqueline S. Johnson and Elissa L. Newport, "Critical Period Effects in Second Language Learning: The Influence of Maturational State on the Acquisition of English as a Second Language," *Cognitive Psychology* 21, no. 1 (1989): 60–99.
4. David Birdsong, ed., *Second Language Acquisition and the Critical Period Hypothesis* (Mahwah, NJ: Erlbaum, 1999).
5. Sarah-Jayne Blakemore and Suparna Choudhury, "Development of the Adolescent Brain: Implications for Executive Function and Social Cognition," *Journal of Child Psychology and Psychiatry* 47, no. 3–4 (2006): 296–312.
6. Rachel Keen, "The Development of Problem Solving in Young Children: A Critical Cognitive Skill," *Annual Review of Psychology* 62, no. 1 (2011): 1–21.

Chapter 6

1. Mark Schneider, "Finishing the First Lap: The Cost of First-Year Student Attrition in America's Four-Year Colleges and Universities," American Institutes for Research, www
.air.org/resource/finishing-first-lap-cost-first-year-student
-attrition-america%E2%80%99s-four-year-colleges-and.
2. Karen Arenson, "Applications to Colleges Are Breaking Records," *New York Times*, www.nytimes.com/2008/01/17
/education/17admissions.html?_r=0.
3. Angela L. Duckworth and Martin E. P. Seligman, "Self-Discipline Outdoes IQ in Predicting Academic Performance of Adolescents," *Psychological Science* 16, no. 12 (2005): 939–44.

4. Robert McCrae and Paul Costa, "Validation of the Five-Factor Model of Personality Across Instruments and Observers," *Journal of Personality and Social Psychology* 15 (1987): 81–90; Erik E. Noftle and Richard Robins, "Personality Predictors of Academic Outcomes: Big Five Correlates of GPA and SAT Scores," *Journal of Personality and Social Psychology* 93, no. 1 (2007): 116–30.

5. "Smart," Dictionary.com, www.dictionary.reference.com.

6. Charles Spearman, "'General Intelligence,' Objectively Determined and Measured," *American Journal of Psychology* 15, no. 2 (1904): 201–91; John B. Carroll, *Human Cognitive Abilities: A Survey of Factor-Analytic Studies* (Cambridge: Cambridge University Press, 1993); Howard E. Gardner, *Intelligence Reframed Multiple Intelligences for the Twenty-First Century* (New York: Basic Books, 2000); Daniel Goleman, *Emotional Intelligence* (New York: Bantam Books, 1995).

Chapter 7

1. Courtnie Packer, "Are Teenagers Becoming Too Attached to Their Cell Phones?" Top Ten Reviews, http://cell-phone -parental-control-software-review.toptenreviews.com/are -teenagers-becoming-too-attached-to-their-cell-phones. html.

2. Dara Kerr, "One-Fifth of Third-Graders Own Cell Phones," CNET, April 9, 2012, www.cnet.com/news/one-fifth-of-third -graders-own-cell-phones/; Mary Madden et al., "Teens and Technology 2013," Pew Research Internet Project, March 13, 2013, www.pewinternet.org/Reports/2013/Teens-and-Tech .aspx.

3. Carolyn Gregoire, "How Technology Is Warping Your Memory," Huffington Post, December 11, 2013, www.huffingtonpost.com/2013/12/11/technology-changes-memory_n_4414778.html.
4. Packer, "Are Teenagers Becoming Too Attached to Their Cell Phones?"
5. Ibid.
6. "Back to School: Choosing a Cell Phone for Your Child," ABC News, August 30, 2010, www.abcnews.go.com/GMA/Parenting/choosing-cell-phone-child/story?id=11510255; Suzanne Kantra, "Android vs iPhone for Kids: How to Choose," USA Today, September 16, 2013, www.usatoday.com/story/tech/personal/2013/09/16/how-to-choose-android-vs-iphone-for-kids/2820029/; Miles Brignall, "Mobile Phones for Children: A Buyer's Guide," Guardian (London), June 6, 2013, www.theguardian.com/money/2013/jun/06/mobile-phones-children-buyers-guide.

Chapter 8

1. Madden et al., "Teens and Technology 2013."
2. Hilary Buff Greenwood, The Relationship between the Qualities of Adolescents' Online Friendship and Experience of Loneliness (San Diego, CA: Alliant International University, 2008).
3. Dara Kerr, "One-Fifth of Third-Graders Own Cell Phones," CNET, April 9, 2012, http://news.cnet.com/8301-1023_3-57411576-93/one-fifth-of-third-graders-own-cell-phones.
4. Oliver Smith, "Facebook Terms and Conditions: Why You Don't Own Your Online Life," Telegraph (London), January 4, 2013, www.telegraph.co.uk/technology/social-media/9780565/Facebook-terms-and-conditions-why-you-dont-own-your-online-life.html.

5. American Academy of Child and Adolescent Psychiatry, "Children and TV Violence," *Facts for Families* no. 13, March 2011, www.aacap.org/App_Themes/AACAP/docs/facts_for _families/13_children_and_tv_violence.pdf.
6. Henry J. Kaiser Family Foundation, "Daily Media Use among Children and Teens Up Dramatically from Five Years Ago," news release, January 20, 2010, www.kff.org/disparities -policy/press-release/daily-media-use-among-children-and -teens-up-dramatically-from-five-years-ago.

Chapter 9
1. "Youth Sports Statistics," Statistic Brain RSS, www .statisticbrain.com/youth-sports-statistics.

Chapter 10
1. Elizabeth Lander, "Teen Brain More Prone to Drug, Alcohol Damage," *The Chart* (blog), CNN, November 15, 2010, http:// thechart.blogs.cnn.com/2010/11/15/teen-brain-more-prone -to-drug-alcohol-damage.
2. Ibid.
3. Mark Gregston, "Drug Abuse Starting Earlier than Ever," OnePlace.com, www.oneplace.com/ministries/parenting-todays- teens-weekend/read/articles/drug-abuse-startingearlier-than- ever-11971.html.
4. "Drug Guide for Parents: Learn Facts to Keep Your Teens Safe" (2010),www.drugfree.org/wp-content/uploads/2010/10/drug _chart_10.25.10_opt.pdf.
5. Centers for Disease Control and Prevention, "Injury Prevention and Control," www.cdc.gov/Motorvehiclesafety /costs/policy.html.
6. Ibid.

7. Teen Drug Addiction, "Welcome to Teen Drug Addiction," www.teendrugaddiction.com.

8. Lander, "Teen Brain More Prone to Drug, Alcohol Damage."

Index

About the Authors

Darlene Sweetland, PhD, is a licensed clinical psychologist with twenty years of experience specializing in work with children, adolescents, and young adults. She has served as head psychologist at a private school for students with learning disorders and clinical director for an agency for individuals with developmental disorders, and she currently maintains a private practice in Del Mar,  California. As a child psychologist, she specializes in working with children and teens struggling with social, academic, and emotional challenges. She is established as a sought-after therapist and speaker in the areas of child and family therapy. Dr. Sweetland is the coauthor of *Intellectual Disability and Mental Health: A Training Manual in Dual Diagnosis* (2011), which has been a primary training guide in psychiatric hospitals and mental health agencies for professionals working with individuals who are dually diagnosed.

Ron Stolberg, PhD, is a licensed clinical psychologist and an associate professor at Alliant International University in San Diego, California. As a family therapist, he specializes in working with children with acting-out behaviors and their families. He has authored numerous chapters published in seminal textbooks in psychology and contributed to a new book: *Therapeutic Assessment with the MMPI-2* (2011). A former psychologist for the hit reality TV show *Survivor*, he currently serves as the president of the board of directors at the Winston School for children struggling with learning disorders. Dr. Stolberg regularly presents at a wide variety of national and international conferences.

Dr. Sweetland and Dr. Stolberg have been married for sixteen years and have two sons. They live in San Diego. They, too, are facing the challenges of raising children in this generation.